CW00551867

The Neolithic henge and stone circle at Avebury are well-known to many people. But few visitors explore the other prehistoric sites nearby in the World Heritage Site. *Beyond the Henge* is a guide to four different walks of between one and six miles which take in all the significant surviving archaeological sites. Three of the walks focus on the Neolithic and Bronze Age monuments while the fourth walk explores Avebury's Anglo-Saxon and medieval origins.

Along the way Bob Trubshaw introduces ideas about the changing lifestyles and beliefs of the prehistoric people who built the monuments. The variety of such ideas currently being proposed by prehistorians are presented using a unique conversational style of writing.

Join Bob Trubshaw and his fictional friend Simon as they set forth from the henge to its precursors on WindmillHill and West Kennett long barrow, then to later monuments such as Silbury Hill. And afterwards visit where the pagan Anglo-Saxons celebrated their rituals – and the first evidence for Christianity in the parish.

Bob Trubshaw has been writing about archaeology, folklore, mythology and local history for nearly twenty-five years. This is his tenth book. He first visited Avebury in 1980 and has lived there since 2010. The routes described in this book have been walked by him many times with a variety of real-life friends.

Beyond the Henge

Exploring Avebury's World Heritage Site

Bob Trubshaw

Heart of Albion

Beyond the Henge:
Exploring Avebury's World Heritage Site
Bob Trubshaw

ISBN 978-1-905646-22-7

Published by
Heart of Albion Press
113 High Street
Avebury
Marlborough
Wiltshire
SN8 1RF

albion@indigogroup.co.uk

Visit our Web site: www.hoap.co.uk

Printed in England by Booksprint

Contents

Preface

A simplified timeline

Before we get started   1

First walk   5

Second walk   41

Third walk   74

Fourth walk   131

Acknowledgements   142

Sources   152

Preface

Writing about prehistoric monuments using the metric system seems really odd to me. So I've used yards and feet – with apologies to all those who never learnt about such units of measurement at school. As it happens a metre is only a little longer than a yard, so no conversion is needed. There are three feet in a yard (so one foot is about 300 mm).

I have mostly changed dates to 'years before present' rather than the convention of BC and AD used by archaeologists. There are a few exceptions where the dating evidence is unusually precise.

The River Kennet is conventionally spelt with on 't' while the villages of East and West Kennett are conventionally spelt with two 't's. As West Kennett long barrow is named after the parish I spell it with two 't's – although archaeologists usually only use one.

This guidebook is intended to be used in conjunction with Ordnance Survey Explorer Map sheet 157 (Avebury and Devizes). Grid references are included for all the key places visited along the routes.

Please do make time to visit the Alexander Keiller Museum at Avebury and see the various archaeological finds, especially the nationally-important ones from Windmill Hill. The museum is in two seventeenth century buildings – the thatched threshing barn and the nearby stables. Avebury is almost unique among prehistoric sites in that finds from excavations are on display in the museum right in the midst of the locations where they were discovered.

Bob Trubshaw

Avebury

July 2012

A simplified timeline

Archaeologists frequently revise their ideas of how old the past might be! These are the dates are currently in favour. Note that these dates apply to *British* prehistory – dates for Continental Europe may be a little earlier. All are approximate (except for the Roman era in England and Wales) and there would have been some overlap of cultures.

Upper Palaeolithic	40,000 to 35,000 to 10,000 BC
Mesolithic	10,000 to 4,000 BC
Early Neolithic	4,000 to 3,000 BC
Late Neolithic	3,000 to 2,200 BC
Early Bronze Age	2,200 to 1,500 BC
Middle Bronze Age	1,500 to 1,200 BC
Late Bronze Age	1,200 to 800 BC
Early Iron Age	800 to 400 BC
Late Iron Age	400 BC to AD 43 (England and Wales)
	400 BC to AD 500 (Scotland and Ireland)
Roman	AD 43 to 410
Anglo-Saxon	AD 410 to 1066

Before we get started

'It's big, isn't it, Bob?'

'What, Simon, the henge? Yes, it's the biggest prehistoric henge and stone circle that has survived. About a quarter a mile across and, following the paths, about a mile or so to walk around. But at the time it was built this was only a small part of what was going on here.'

'What do you mean? There's more to Avebury than the henge? I thought that was the main attraction'

'Well most people who come here are happy just to stroll around the henge. But since 1986 it has been part of a UNESCO World Heritage Site which stretches more than a mile in each direction.

'Look over there – can you just make out the top of Windmill Hill? That's one of the places where it all started and that's about a mile-and-a-half away. Look the opposite way at the other side of that hill looking somewhat like a beached whale – that's Waden Hill – and beyond there is Silbury Hill, also over a mile away. Beyond Silbury Hill are places like West Kennett chamber tomb and the rather odd site known as the Sanctuary.

'And look over the Marlborough Downs and the Ridgeway. Each of those clumps of beech trees is hiding one or more Bronze Age barrows, which were built quite a bit after the henge.'

'So it wasn't all built at one time then?'

'Far from it. The earliest earthworks on Windmill Hill and the chamber tombs such as West Kennett were several hundred years before anything we known for certain about

Opposite: *Standing on the bank of the south-west sector just before sunset, looking across to the south circle. The eastern entrance is in the middle, hidden by the trees.*

Looking north from the south entrance. The arrow points to Windmill Hill. Although the trees now conceal Windmill Hill, without them it would be visible from anywhere in the henge.

the henge itself. Silbury Hill wasn't built until right at the end of the Neolithic. After that there are the Bronze Age barrows, a Roman town, and all sorts of evidence for the Anglo-Saxons.'

'A Roman town – but I never seen that.'

'Well no, apart from some geofiz plots and a few small trenches no one has. At least since whenever it all fell down, presumably well before the Norman Conquest. But I could take you and show you where it was.'

'What about the other places you mentioned? Can you show me those too Bob?'

'Well Simon in some cases I can only show you where they were. But yes, there are footpaths that go to or near everywhere of interest.'

''We can't drive there?'

'Mostly not. You really need to be able to walk. If you wanted to visit all of them in a day you'd end up walking well over twelve miles… '

'I can't do that!'

2

'Me neither. But can you do five or six miles today, and the same again tomorrow, bearing in mind it won't be some sort of race and there will be plenty of stopping and looking?'

'Yes, so long as it's not all uphill.'

'No, there's a gentle climb up to Windmill Hill and a couple of short but steep-ish paths on Waden Hill and the Ridgeway. But nothing really strenuous.'

'Well, how about we do one of these five or six milers today and the other one tomorrow?'

'Sounds good to me. But before we finish today I'll also need to have a good look at the henge.'

'Shall we do it now?'

'We could. But it might make more sense if we go first to one of the places where it all started – Windmill Hill – and then come back to the henge, so we experience it in chronological order, so to speak.'

'OK, that's fine by me. But if we're going walk about six miles then we're going to be gone at least a couple of hours.'

'Frankly, we need to allow at least three hours. Unless we time it right when the Waggon and Horses at Beckhampton is open then there's nowhere to get a drink or food, and not much that offers any shelter if it starts to rain.'

'Hmmm. So we need lots of chocolate!'

'Maybe, but chocolate tends to melt on a day like today. I take usually take apples, dried fruit such as dates or figs, and some nuts. And a bottle of water, of course. Or we could take sandwiches.'

'Does the shop in the High Street sell those sort of things?'

'Oh yes! Say, what if I get stocked up while you go back to your car and get your walking boots and a waterproof?'

'Won't these shoes do? And it doesn't look in the least like rain!'

'We'll be walking through a lot of pasture fields, with grass about ankle deep, sometimes deeper. It tends to trap the moisture so those shoes will just get sodden and you'll end walking most of the way with soggy socks. Which would probably mean some interesting blisters.'

'Get your point.'

'And no matter what the weather's doing now, this is England. Have you ever thought that it might be windy on top of a place called Windmill Hill? And wet and windy quickly means wet, windy and cold.'

'OK, OK, you know best. Better to be safe than sorry.'

'I've got the Ordnance Survey map – the 1:25,000 Explorer series is really good. And just for once Avebury is about in the middle of the sheet.'

'Do you need it to find the paths?'

'Perhaps not, as I know this area well. But unless you really do know the whole area like the back of your hand then the map is really useful for working out all the places you can see on the skyline round and about.'

'Good point. Maps aren't just for finding our where you are, they tell you where you're not. If that makes sense'

'Just about! Yes, they're brilliant for getting to understand the landscape and how the different places fit together. You can't really understand a landscape just from a map – you really do have to be there too – but 'just being there' makes more sense when you have a map too!'

'And before you ask, Bob, yes I've got my camera and my mobile!'

'Good, good. Meet you back here on near the village shop in ten minutes then.'

Checklist for walks

Waterproof boots
Waterproof jacket or cagoule
Hat and gloves in winter
Food and water; thermos with hot drink in winter
Ordnance Survey map
Camera
Mobile phone

Firrt walk

This walk is about five or six miles and will take about three hours. The first part requires negotiating at least six stiles.

The starting point is in Avebury High Street by the end of the main path from the visitors' car park (grid reference 101699). See map on page 10.

'Hi again Simon! Let's set off down the High Street. This bit here goes through the original western entrance to the henge and is where the pairs of megaliths making up the Beckhampton Avenue ended. That wooden building with a mossy corrugated roof – it was still thatched in the 1930s – and that cottage on the end of the row of four are both where the henge bank used to be. The back gardens of the

The buildings at the start of this walk.

Pasture V

the ---- 1719

Pasture VIII

1717

1717

1713

1715

1718

1714

A

Pasture III

Pasture II

6

two cottages in the middle are in the henge ditch. The one on the right is where the stones would have been. But I'll explain more about the henge and the Avenues as we go around.'

'But rather than follow the High Street, we need to turn off into the churchyard. This rather attractive lychgate has a scallop shell carved in the wood... '

'Oh yes! Why's that?'

'Because the church is dedicated to St James and he is most famously associated with the pilgrimage route to Santiago in north-west Spain. And medieval pilgrims who had been there came back with a scallop shell as a souvenir.'

'The church itself looks rather interesting.'

'Indeed. There's parts of the building that are tenth or eleventh century.'

'You mean it was built before the Norman Conquest?'

'Well everything you can see from this side is all a few centuries later. But, yes, the oldest parts are Anglo-Saxon. I'll bring you back here when we've done our walk.

[See the Fourth Walk on page 131.]

'I thought Avebury was all about the prehistoric.'

'Well, there's all that, of course. But there's more as well!'

'Let's head over there to the west and that little gateway.'

Grid reference 099699

'This wall on our right is the boundary of the gardens of Avebury Manor. The oldest part of the house is sixteenth century.'

'Can we go in sometime?'

'Yes. I'll need to check when the opening hours are but the gardens are usually open in daytime even when the house isn't.

Opposite: *Avebury as drawn by William Stukeley in 1724. Without Stukeley's many drawings and aerial views much less would be known about the prehistoric stones. The letter 'A' has been added to indicate the buildings which are now the Henge Shop and Manor Farm.*

The west side of the churchyard with the upper floors of Avebury Manor visible over the boundary wall.

At the time of publication Avebury Manor is closed on Weds and open the other six days from 11 a.m. to 5 p.m.. But check online or at the Barn Gallery of the Alexander Keiller Museum.

'The oldest bit of the building seems to be sixteenth century, although it was added to several times until the eighteenth century. But there seems to have been a house on the site in the thirteenth century. And it's quite likely that the origins are in the early twelfth century, during the reign of Henry I, when the abbey of St George de Boscherville, which is near Rouen in France, founded a small priory there. This was quite separate to the church.

Grid reference 097699
'This little bridge is neat. Is it modern?'
          'Well most of what you can see is modern. But one span is

old. It seems it was always only a few feet wide. We're standing over the Winterbourne. As the name suggests, it normally only flows during the winter and usually dries out during the summer and autumn.

'Look that way – there's Windmill Hill, where we're heading. But turn around. There's Silbury Hill, where we'll get to later. And until the seventeenth century the Beckhampton Avenue – a double row of stones just like the West Kennet Avenue – went across this meadow parallel to our east-west path about a hundred yards away.'

'But I can't see anything… '

''No, all the stones were buried or broken up.'

'How far did it go?'

'Ah ha – I'll show you exactly where when we come down from Windmill Hill. A pair of stones associated with the end of the Avenue still stand.

'Keep to the right where the path forks, then hop over the stile a few yards along on the right.

Grid reference 096699; see photograph on page 12.

'You've got it, now head to that little wooden bridge slightly to the right.'

'This one is modern. But why are we crossing the Winterbourne again?'

'We're not! This is known as the Horslip Brook or the Sambourn. When you've finished crossing just step a bit to your right.

Grid reference 097700

'Ah! Yes, it's as if we're in the point of a triangle. The two little rivers meet here.'

'The posh name is a "confluence". All sorts of ritual and religious sites are built in these places, especially where bigger rivers meet, from the Bronze Age right through into the medieval period. Indeed when the water flowing here finally joins the River Thames it does so where Henry I founded Reading Abbey in just such a confluence.

'I think it's interesting that Windmill Hill – the oldest of the Avebury prehistoric monuments – sits at the wide end of the

9

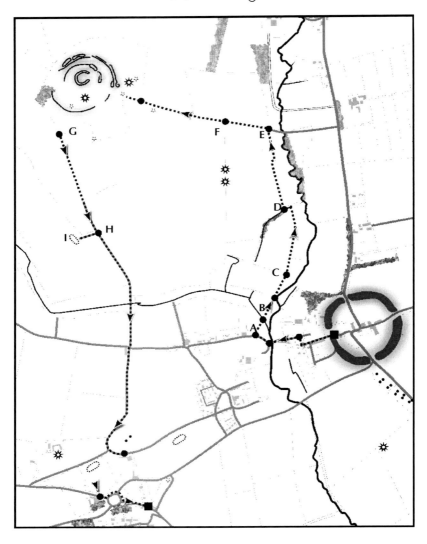

Letters refer to the stiles and gates marked in the photographs on the following pages.

triangle you described, between these two seasonal streams. And the slightly later henge is to the east side of the Winterbourne on an area of higher ground before the ground drops away to what is now a dry valley. And Silbury Hill is very closely linked to where the Winterbourne meets an important spring, called Swallowhead, and then changes its direction and name to the Kennet. But that'll make more sense when we get there.'

'So you think this relationship of all these prehistoric monuments to the local watercourses is not just accidental?'

'Probably not. But don't ask me what they really meant by it all as there are no clear clues!'

'Where are we going now?'

Grid reference 098701

'Can you see a gap in the hedge over on the far side of the field? There's a stile there. This part of the walk takes us over a series of stiles. Sometimes it's hard to see where they are but looking carefully at the grass usually reveals a subtle change in colour where other people have walked before.'

'Ah, got it – it's quite subtle. It's clearer in the distance than close up!'

'Try to keep to that path. Partly because you'll minimise any damage to the grass – especially as it grows longer than it is now – but also because you'll help to keep the wear-path showing clearly for other people.'

Grid references for the stiles are 098702 and 098707

'Interestingly I set off along this path about noon one day not long before midwinter and found myself with my shadow laid out in front of me all the way.'

'So we're heading due north. It seems we're walking more or less alongside the Winterbourne.'

Directions to the path start again on page 20 . During this part of the walk Bob and Simon discuss what life might have been like in prehistoric England.

Photographs of the route appear on the following pages.

'Yes. Windmill Hill is still somewhat to our left rather than straight ahead. When we finally get to a farm track we'll turn left to climb up to the summit.'

'When did people first come up here?'

'Well, we know that people were in the valleys and coombs close to here during the Mesolithic.'

'Now, that's what was once called the "Middle Stone Age" – after the Old Stone Age and before the New Stone Age.'

'Indeed, Paleolithic, Mesolithic and Neolithic are just the Latin words for Old, Middle and New Stone Ages.'

'So the children of Paleolithic parents grew up into Mesolithic people?'

'No. The children of Mesolithic parents probably grew up to be Neolithic people – although there is a little bit of controversy about that – but there is a complete gap between Paleolithic people and Mesolithic people.;

'Why's that?'

'A not-so little event called the last Ice Age. A bit further north of here and there were glaciers many hundreds of feet thick. Here in Wiltshire there weren't any glaciers but the

12

soil was permanently frozen, with just the top few inches melting in the summer.'

'So, permafrost – as they have in Siberia and such places.'

'Exactly. It was the melt waters from the permafrost which almost certainly created the dry valleys or coombs around here. Once the permafrost had gone then water could drain away through the chalk. But while the chalk was frozen then streams formed in the summer and they caused erosion.'

'And no one lived here then?'

'Certainly any humans who had being living in the British Isles before the Ice Age didn't hang around. Perhaps they were able to wander off to somewhere less challenging, but maybe they just didn't make it through an especially bad patch of weather. Only when the Ice Age begins to abate and the glaciers start to melt do people come back.'

'Presumably at that time this part of the world would be a bit like Greenland or northern Scandinavia is today.'

'I suppose that's a reasonable comparison. If it's true then it would give an idea of the sort of animals they might be hunting, and what other resources they would be exploiting. However the evidence we have for the Mesolithic elsewhere in Britain suggests they were hunting deer, and collecting shell fish and hazel nuts in seemingly "industrial" quantities. So, even if things start out a bit like Greenland, within a few thousand years they are much more like say Scotland in recent times.'

'How many thousand years ago are we talking about. Every time I read a book on archaeology they seem to give different dates,'

> 'Yes, indeed. Archaeologists have changed their minds about "how old is old" in a big way at least twice in my lifetime. And they're still tweaking things. With the Mesolithic in Britain you're fairly safe if you think from 12,000 till 6,000 years before now. But in Europe the Mesolithic starts before then, as the Ice Age has a bit less impact on people's lives.

'What makes the Mesolithic people different from the people who came after, the Neolithic folk?'

> 'Two or three things stand out. But they're all really big things! In three words "farming, pottery, monuments".'

'Mesolithic people weren't farmers then?'

'No. They are known as "hunter-gatherers". Presumably the women spent a lot of time gathering and the blokes occasionally went off on hunting trips, so perhaps it would be better to call them "gatherers and hunters". But nobody does, the term "hunter-gatherer" has stuck. Whatever, they were migratory. They presumably spent different times of the year in different places, though whether they came back to exactly the same places each year or instead had a choice of 'spring time' places and a choice of 'autumn time' places is an open question.'

'So a bit like Gypsies?'

'I think we have to be cautious about making modern-day comparisons. But some of the work done by people recording the lives of the Scottish Travellers in the 1960s suggests that – despite that by then they were traders and tinkers – their traditional routes across the Scottish Highlands were at least something like how we might expect hunter-gatherers to have travelled around many millennia before.'

'So are the Scottish Travellers the distant descendants of Mesolithic people?'

'That would be taking things a little too far I think. There's no evidence to support it – but then again there's no evidence

to say that it is impossible! But direct continuity seems unlikely.'

'Farming is clearly quite different to nomadic lifestyles. You need to be in one place to tend crops and even animals.'

'Maybe. And maybe not. Archaeologists used to assume that a bunch of people arrived from the Continent with their ideas of farming and somehow pushed the hunter-gathering people further and further into the hills and other places less suited to farming. But perhaps the reality was less clear cut. Perhaps the people here saw the benefits of the new way of doing things and quickly adapted. What is clear is that the domesticated animals – cattle and the sheep-goats – all originated in the Middle East.

'Did you say sheep *and* goats?'

'No, I just called them "sheep-goats". It's very hard to tell which is which from the bones – it's better not worry too much about the difference. Even the sheep would have had much longer legs and smaller bodies than the sort of animals that have been bred in the last three hundred years.

'Interestingly, one of the few Neolithic animal skeletons which can be identified as a goat rather than a sheep was found on Windmill Hill and is on display in the Stables Gallery museum. They also have the complete bones of a Neolithic pig and a dog.

'What they weren't doing is keeping the livestock in fenced-off fields. Think of it more like ranching than modern farming.'

'A bit like the way Sámi people follow and manage their reindeer herds?'

'That's perhaps a reasonable comparison.'

'And ranching would make sense too for the cattle – a bit like the ranches in the American Mid West that I remember from cowboy movies!'

'Well Hollywood movies about the nineteenth century Wild West don't tell us much about life in Britain five thousand years ago!'

'But the cattle were domesticated versions of the wild cattle that were living in the British Isles during the Mesolithic?'

'No, not at all. Neolithic domesticated cattle are much smaller than the native wild cattle. As I said, these were breeds that had been domesticated in the Middle East several thousand years before they made it all the way over here. The indigenous European cattle – often called aurochs – were very big with huge horns. A few herds still survive in eastern Europe and they're not at all friendly to humans. No one has succeeded in domesticating them. We've no idea of how the smaller and more docile cattle breeds came about, but they're very different to aurochs. When we go into the Barn Gallery of the museum remind me to show you the two ankle bones – one from an aurochs and one from a domesticated Neolithic cattle. The difference in size is really striking!

'Did they domesticate pigs too?'

'Perhaps. Wild pigs were hunted and, at some point, become more "domesticated". In the wild they mostly live in woodland so do not compete for the grass grazed by cows and sheep. Pigs are every good at using their tusks to turn over the soil, so would have been very helpful to early farmers who didn't have proper ploughs.'

'Were any other animals domesticated?'

'Well, not for food. But dogs seem to have become man's best friend very early on – seemingly in the Mesolithic. It may well be that humans didn't domesticate dogs but more than dogs domesticated themselves… '

'They are scavengers after all, so humans would have been a handy source of scraps.'

'And a warming fire too. And once people start "ranching" animals then trained dogs become very useful, if only to fend off wolves and other predators. It is easy to see some sort of symbiotic relationship quickly benefiting both dogs and humans.'

'But I think of farming as less about animals as growing crops.'

'Indeed. And grain crops – using species which are not native to Britain but which are first cultivated in the Middle East – are exactly what we begin to see in the Neolithic. And here on the chalk downland we are in the midst of countryside which – until the invention of artificial fertilisers about sixty years ago brought about so many changes to British farming – was noted for raising sheep and growing corn. And without the sheep – or, more pedantically, the sheep dung – there would be no corn crops.'

'It's the sheep that fertilise the fields for the corn.'

'Yes, chalk lets nutrients quickly wash away. And that was just as true in the Neolithic as was now.

'So because we've domesticated sheep we can start to grow corn and eat bread?'

'Maybe. But the easiest way to get the nutrients out of grain is to boil it up rather than go to all the trouble of grinding it into flour.'

'Oh, so gruel and porridge… Ughh!'

'And something part-way to rice pudding if you make it with milk and a little bit of honey! But interestingly any left over gruel and such like will turn to a beer-like liquid within a week.'

'That sounds much more fun!'

'Yes, we have to imagine that the gatherings up here on Windmill Hill changed from teetotal affairs in the Mesolithic to somewhat more Club 18-30 events in the Neolithic.'

'What else did you say distinguished the Neolithic – pottery? That would be handy for the beer brewing and drinking.'

'Yes! The Mesolithic people made clever use of flint for their tools. They used wood, hides and presumably many other natural substances. But the oldest fired pottery vessels are from the same Middle Eastern sites where there is evidence of domesticated animals. So in some sense there is a "Neolithic package" of domesticated animals, cultivated plants and pottery.'

'Which the Neolithic people brought with them as they took over all the best land for farming, leaving the Mesoliothic people had to go and hunt and gather in places which were no good for farming.'

'That's what archaeologists used to think. Then they changed their minds and realised that Neolithic people might still get up to a bit of hunting and fishing themselves.'

'Just like some farmer in the mid-western American Prairies has a day off from driving his tractor and puts a hunting rifle or fishing rods in the back of his station wagon and heads off into the woods and such like to get some deer or fish to stock up his freezer?'

'Maybe, and maybe not. But more importantly, the archaeologists realised that the Mesolithic people here first weren't daft and could easily learn how to farm and make pots. You didn't need a whole "invasion" of Neolithic people – just a few people to show the way, so to speak.'

'That's like the way people in Britain and elsewhere now eat beefburgers, drink cola, wear denim trousers, watch Hollywood movies, listen to country and western music and so forth. It's not because we've been invaded by lots of Americans, it's because the people living here decide it's a good thing to do.'

'Well, at least some people do! But, yes, the material culture you leave behind for future archaeologists reveals more about your aspirations than about where you were born, or even your parents' lifestyles.'

'So it was less of a Neolithic invasion than the Mesolithic people learning new ways of living.'

'Yes – and perhaps also sometimes no! Imagine a whole mix from a few people who did indeed immigrate, some old die-hards who wanted to keep to the old ways, and a mix of in-between folk who adapted more or less slowly, and to a greater or lesser extent.'

'Much like today then.'

'Well five thousand years might sound like a long time but, changes in technology and culture excepted, there's no reason to think of people then as much different to us. They might have been a bit more resourceful and used to living in what would seem to us a harsh life-style but they'd tick along pretty much the same otherwise.'

After about half a mile.

Grid reference 097711

'Right, over this stile – it's the last one – and turn left to that gate. It's got a tricky catch on it, you might need to find a stone to give it a thump. This gentle slope is the eastern side of Windmill Hill. In the field to our left is flint and pottery from all through the Neolithic period. It seems this is south slope is where people camped year after year.'

'Camped rather than lived?'

'Yes, it seems most likely. Although it's hard to prove anything, the best guess is that people got together here for a few days or weeks at a time for a mixture of religious and social reasons. A study of the teeth of cattle found at other causewayed enclosures suggests that they were mostly killed in August or September.'

'And the area of high ground around Avebury – about five hundred feet above sea level – is in just the right place for people to get together each year as it's between three important river systems.'

'Three rivers? But you've only mentioned the Winterbourne and the Kennet… '

'Remember the Kennet flows into the Thames at Reading. And not very far to our west the land drops sharply away to places like Chippenham and Wooton Bassett which are above the valley of the River Avon – the one that comes from around Stratford upon Avon and goes through Gloucester and Bristol and such like.

'And to the south of here, near Bishops Cannings, is the end of a valley which drops into the Vale of Pewsey. That's the vale created by various streams which come together to form a different River Avon. This one flows into the Solent at Christchurch. Places such as Pewsey and Salisbury straddle it. Interestingly it goes close to Stonehenge – and even closer to another major prehistoric henge site at Marden.'

'Marden? Never heard of that one!'

'Not too many people have although it's roughly the same size as Avebury and other so-called 'mega henges' such as the one at Dorchester. No stones survive and not a lot of archaeology has been done there. But it is just about exactly half-way between Stonehenge and Avebury.'

'In my way of thinking it was easier to get about in the Neolithic by a little boat than it was by walking. This would be especially true if you were carrying a lot of food and other stuff – and you'd need to bring all your own food to a gathering here on Windmill Hill as there wouldn't be any way of feeding everybody for very long.'

'Did they have boats then?'

'Yes – quite a few Neolithic "log boats" have been found in places like the River Trent. And it's clear that people had been getting from island to island around Scotland by boat for several thousand years before than. By the time of the Neolithic we'd been messing about in boats for a great many generations.

'So I like to think that here on Windmill Hill people would be coming up from the Thames estuary, and maybe from the Cotswolds valleys that also feed into the Thames. They would be meeting up with friends and relatives who'd come up from what we think of as Hampshire and other folks who'd come up from the Bristol and Somerset area. But we have to assume people came from a whole lot of places along the south coast. There is clear evidence from here at Windmill Hill of very early pots made on the Lizard peninsula in south Cornwall, and a fragment of polished axe found by the henge was made from rock only found on the Lizard.

'Once the gathering was over everybody would go back towards their different river valleys.'

'Can you prove it?'

'No! But there is plenty of evidence that Neolithic people kept cattle – and while they can graze on upland areas in the summer, they are much more suited to lower and wetter places, especially during the winter. Up here on the chalk downs there would have been flocks of sheep-goats, and they may have been here all year.'

'And maybe corn?'

'Quite probably. Standing here looking down this south sloping field – it's still being ploughed for arable today – and you're looking down over many millennia of farming. This was the slope where everyone camped.'

'And, from what you were saying about people mixing up farming with more nomadic hunter-gathering , all these folk following their different ways would get together one or more times a year at places such as here. And when they got together they would be sharing ideas just as much as they were trading food, tools, pots, hides, and whatever.'

'I think you're spot on about sharing ideas. But you need to be careful about the word "trade".'

'Well, OK, they didn't have coins so it would have been all about bartering… '

'Maybe, maybe not entirely. Food, pots, hides and all the rest undoubtedly had practical value and could be swapped for other necessities. But they may well have had another value too depending on whether they were regarded as "high status".'

'The same way some people need to be seen with the latest model of mobile phone, even though an old one would still make phone calls just as well?'

'Yes. But while prehistoric people just might have had a notion of bling, the most important thing you can do with a high status item is give it away.'

'Eh? But if I've just got my hands on the latest mobile phone I'm not likely to give it away… '

'Really? What if you gave it to the girl of your dreams… '

'She might want to, well, you know… '

'Indeed. Gifts are partly about being seen to be generous but mostly about what you expect in return. At the very least there is an obligation to make a gift of similar "value". So what if your tribal leader gave a high status item to you?'

'I guess I'd owe him some sort of big favour… '

'Spot on. And I suspect that when folk got together up here then an awful lot of gifts were exchanged.'

'A bit like a big family get-together at Christmas with presents everywhere… '

'Well I don't expect archaeologists will ever find any prehistoric wrapping paper with Santas printed on it! But I

One of the Bronze Age barrows on the summit of Windmill Hill.

suppose you might be right. I'm tempted to think more about a few "big" presents rather than lots of little ones. A useful quantity of hides or corn rather than new socks and boxes of sweets... But then as now it was all about *who* you needed to give gifts to – and who you expected to get gifts *from* – that was key to the whole event. People needed to be seen being generous. And all sorts of reciprocal obligations ensued'

'OK, so perhaps not trade as we think of it. Can I call it "wealth exchange"?'

'That's pretty much what an academic would call it. It's nice and vague about the "how" while realising that what goes on is fairly crucial to the way the society works.'

'Back there you said there were three things that distinguish the Neolithic from the Mesolithic. You've discussed the farming and the pottery. What was the third?'

'Monuments.'

'Ah yes, I remember. What's the big deal about them?'

'Well they all start right here – and a few other places like Windmill Hill.'

Grid reference 089714

'OK, now we're almost at the top. Just step through this gateway. What you can see right in front of you is a prehistoric monument. Only it's not Neolithic, and certainly not Mesolithic. You're looking at a Bronze Age burial mound, or barrow.

'And the Bronze Age comes after the end of the Neolithic... '

'Yes. The person – or persons – buried here lived about four thousand years ago. These are a fine group of Bronze Ages barrows. We need to go over to the right to see what's left of the oldest prehistoric monument up here.

'The Neolithic earthworks up here were excavated in the 1920s by Alexander Keiller. He was an amateur archaeologist but set higher standards of excavation than the professionals of his time. The excavations here were the first detailed look at the lives of early Neolithic people. Indeed, until at least the 1970s the early Neolithic was known as "Windmill Hill Culture", although that name has been dropped now.

'After he'd finished here Keiller excavated in Avebury Avenue and then the henge – and founded the museum there which is named after him.'

'What's so special about causewayed enclosures?'

'They're special because they are among the very first prehistoric monuments. It's the first time people start modifying the landscape in permanent ways. Before that the most radical thing people were doing was clearing large areas of woodland – probably by burning. We take digging up and piling up earth and such like for granted. We forget that if you think of the landscape as the body of a goddess then digging into her is a ritual activity.

'I can't say that I really think of the land as a goddess. That's a bit too flaky and New Agey for me.'

'Well I'm not suggesting that prehistoric people had the same views as New Age folk. But throughout the world –

The more conspicuous 'ditches' on Windmill Hill are actually the result of fairly recent quarrying for chalk. But they follow the ditches of the early Neolithic causewayed enclosure.

certainly throughout modern day rural China – thinking of the land as a body is the natural "common sense" way of thinking. And it's not simply a metaphorical way of thinking – it really is a "lived experience," so to speak.'

'So Mesolithic and Neolithic people are coming here, meeting up, at a place where they really believe they are walking on their goddess?'

'If only I could say that's true for certain. But all comparisons with traditional cultures around the world would suggest that it's the best guess.'

'How big is that goddess?'

'I really only guessing but perhaps there was one goddess for each river valley. Or at least different stretches of longer rivers. There are various River Severns in Britain and each one is named after a goddess whose original name was more like 'Sabrina'. Interestingly, Savernake Forest to the west of here, through which the River Kennet flows on its way towards the Thames, just might be derived from 'Severn' too. Maybe the Kennet is named after a goddess too, although there are several other possible origins.'

The early Neolithic earthworks on the summit of Windmill Hill.

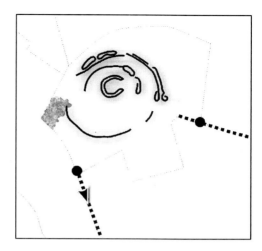

'Why are you so sure it was a goddess and not a god?'

'Everything we know about Iron Age religion suggests they thought the sky was a god and the land was a goddess. There's no reason to think much had changed over the previous thousand or so years.

'The Ancient Egyptians had it the other way about.'

'Indeed. But we're rather a long way from Egypt... '

'Here we are. Except we're not. What looks like a prehistoric ditch is actually recent quarrying. But the original parts of this ditch and the remains of the bank are to all intents and purposes just over five and a half thousand years old. The ditch gently curves around, "enclosing" the summit. There were various gaps – or "causeways" in the ditch.'

'So if we follow this ditch we'll circle the top of the hill.'

'Well, if the ditches still existed we could! Now only some of the ditch here is visible. And even then it's very hard to make out on the ground. If you want to see a causewayed enclosure in more like its original state then one of the best is just over fives miles to the south of here, at Knapp Hill above Alton Priors. It's just hidden over the skyline to the south.'

'But originally the ditches were big enough to be defensive?'

'Probably not. A hundred years ago archaeologists thought they were for defence but it doesn't really seem to fit.

Knapp Hill is one of the best preserved Neolithic causewayed enclosures. Walking around is the nearest you'll get to being back in the early Neolithic.

'Intriguingly one of the reasons why Neolithic causewayed enclosures rarely survive is that the sites were often taken over by Iron Age hill forts – which have much deeper ditches and most certainly were intended for defence. Rybury Hill, just a bit further than Knap Hill, is an example where part of the early Neolithic causewayed enclosure survives, but most of what can be seen is Iron Age.'

'So, originally at least, a causewayed enclosure was a big almost-circular ditch with some gaps in to let people through – and presumably animals too, from what you were saying. Especially if the ditch and bank kept the animals in.'

'If only it were that simple! Maybe the bank had some sort of wattle fence on top. But there's more going on here than just penning up animals and meeting up with the relatives.'

'Such as?'

'For a start, they kept back-filling the ditches and digging new ones. It was more an ongoing activity than "build it and just use it". And also people brought some of the bones of their ancestors up here and placed them in the soil collecting in the ditches.'

'*Some* of the bones? What happened to the rest of the bones?'

'Good question! Look over there to the left of Silbury Hill, about in line with the "shelf" near the summit – can you see West Kennett long barrow?'

'Just a thin darker shape... '

'That's it! Doesn't look that impressive from here but it is one of the biggest of the surviving long barrows – about a hundred yards long. The so-called "burial chamber" is to the left as we're looking at it – it's facing almost due east. That's one of the best of the surviving long barrows around here, but about a thirty others are known within a few miles of here, though only a few can now be seen. One of the lost ones was on the slope of this hill, just near the path – we'll go there shortly. Another was over on the slopes of the Marlborough Downs, at a place shown on the map as Mill Lane. It was near Windmill House which you can just make out from here if you use the map to get bearings. It is referred to by archaeologists as Millbarrow. But the chances are that many more were destroyed before they ever came to the attention of antiquarians or archaeologists.

Grid reference for Millbarrow: approx. 104725

'At the same time in the early Neolithic people were starting to construct these causewayed camps they also started building these long barrows, at least in areas close to the River Severn and the Cotswolds. They seem to fall into two broad types – one type with stone, or sometimes timber, chambers inside which were used for funeral rituals, and another type which are about the same size but don't have chambers and seem not to have any human remains.'

'So some are "chamber tombs" and some are long barrows?'

'It's not quite that simple. At one time archaeologists called them all "chambers tombs". That's before the realised that about half of those they know about never had chambers or even human remains. Now they call them either "chambered long barrows" or, when there is no chamber, "earthen long barrows". But the word "tomb" has been dropped.'

'Even for the ones where there were burials?'

'None of the them ever had burials!'

'But you just said that people were buried in the chambers... '

'No I didn't! I said that the chamber were used for funeral rituals... '

'Isn't that the same thing, just put very pompously?'

'Not at all. A burial has to be buried. The bodies in West Kennett – and other chamber tombs so far as we know – were never buried. They were just laid on the floor of the chamber.'

'Ugh! That sounds gruesome!'

'Maybe. If traditional cultures around the world are any guide then people would only enter the chambers once in the year – the rest of the time it would be taboo to go there.'

'A bit like medieval Christians used to honour the dead at the feasts of All Hallows and All Souls – which after the Reformation became Halloween?'

'There is every reason to think that the church took over an annual ritual which went back many millennia to the time of these barrows.'

'Can you prove that?'

'No! But you can't disprove it either! What's really interesting is that once the bodies had fully decomposed the bones were placed in a fairly organised way in the chambers. Or at least most of the bones. But there is a shortage of skulls and some long bones. Whereas up here on Windmill Hill the excavations revealed skulls and some long bones in the ditches. And, even more curiously, the long bones are mostly from the right leg or arm, rather than the left.

'So far as I can work out from the excavation reports the human bones that were found amount to thirteen skulls or lower jaws, five arms, eight legs and some vertebrae. Presumably there are more in the unexcavated areas.

'So, instead of being buried and – to some extent at least – forgotten, the Neolithic people had a much more complicated way of doing funeral rituals. It's like they had a whole process to go through –

A spiritus – the soul of the deceased – on an eighteenth century monument in Avebury church.

defleshing, initial burial, stacking up the bones, perhaps bringing the skulls to Windmill Hill. And it's almost as if by bringing Grandad's skull up here he's still coming to the "party".'

> 'If only you could prove that! But it's a world-wide belief that the soul resides in the skull. We have almost the same idea today when we think that our "consciousness" is in our brains – indeed modern ideas of ideas of consciousness emerge fairly seamlessly out of traditional ideas of souls. However modern Western thinking does not hold that the bones also have a soul.'

'Indeed. That would be odd.'

> 'But not to most traditional societies. And not really to medieval Christians either. They believed that their bodies would be reunited with their souls at the Final Judgement. So there is some sense that for medieval Christians their bones too had some sense of "identity" after death. So it is well within the realms of plausibility that Neolithic people thought of a "bone soul" as well as what I think of as the "breath soul". Modern Western society is unusual in thinking of only one soul – most cultures, including the Chinese, think of two and sometimes more souls.'

'So, whatever was going up on this headland we know call Windmill Hill, wasn't just about giving gifts and having a good time. It was also a place of your ancestors – or at least their skulls.'

'Yes, rather interesting that you called it a "headland"! It is of course just that, in a topological sense. But I can't help wondering if in the language of the Neolithic the sort of hills on which they created causewayed camps were thought of as the "places of the heads".'

'Oh, that would be an interesting "coincidence". And the circular shape of the ditches is a bit like a skull which has been chopped across.'

'A skull made into a drinking vessel? There's no evidence for that from the Neolithic although there is from the Bronze Age and Iron Age. But if you look at the shape of early pots they are round-bottomed and rather like skull bowls. And at a causewayed enclosure in Cambridgeshire they found inverted round-bottomed pots in just the sort of places where human skulls are found in other such enclosures.'

'So the ritual brew of beer you mentioned could have been served from an ancestor's skull?'

'Or a pot which symbolised an ancestor's skull… '

'Oh, errr! That would reach emotional places that no lager ever could… '

'And remember what I said about the land being the "ultimate" ancestor – the goddess from whom our bodies are borrowed. What if you were drinking from the skull of a grandparent while believing you were inside the skull of the ancestral goddess, the sovereign of the land all around?

'Anyway, we're just speculating. Let's stop all this headspace stuff and just look around us for a moment. What I find really interesting about Windmill Hill is that we feel we're on the top of a modest-sized hill. The skyline seems a fair way off. Yet if you were to go to Knoll Down – over there towards the west, near the obelisk – you'd find yourself looking down on this part of the world. The same from the Ridgeway running along the top of the Marlborough Downs over there to the south and east.'

'It's as if Windmill Hill sits like an upturned saucer between these ridges.'

'Along with Waden Hill, near the henge.'

'Ah, yes, I can see it. Can't make out the henge though.'

No, it's lost in the trees. Look for the tower of Avebury church and it's to the right.

'Even the church tower is surprisingly hard to spot... Pass the map so I can get some bearings. Ah, got it!'

'And then remember that all these ridges and hills are just part of an upland area. Everything drops away sharply to the west into the area around Chippenham. And to the south – beyond Knoll Down – is where the Wansdyke runs along the skyline, just before everything drops down into the Vale of Pewsey.'

'The Wansdyke – that's Anglo-Saxon isn't it?'

'Well most of what we see is, as is the name. But some of the earthworks might date back to the Bronze Age, and the Romans seem to have taken an interest in the earliest bits too.'

'Wiltshire's counterpart to Hadrian's Wall?'

'Probably nothing like as important. But if you want to tax goods and animals being moved about then such a barrier would be helpful. What we can see now probably dates to the end of the eighth century when the Wessex kingdom here was trying to hold off their rivals the Mercians. They had a battle at Kempsford, on the Thames to the south-east of Cirencester, in 802. The Mercians were defeated and it seems only then did this part of the county north of the Wansdyke become part of Wiltshire.'

'Well that makes sense, because the name Wiltshire comes from Wilton-shire, and Wilton is the town near Salisbury in the south of the county.'

'Indeed, Wilton tends to be overlooked because once Salisbury was created in the thirteenth century it lost out to its new big neighbour. But it was the county town for many centuries. Interestingly, Wilton itself takes its name from the River Wylye, a tributary of the Avon.'

'While we're talking about the Saxons, look over to the north. There's a track which circles around the ground below Windmill Hill nearer to the edge of the escarpment. It's easier to work out where it goes from the OS map… '

'Got it! It's called the Herepath. Is that because it was made by hares?'

'No. It's because it was made by the *here*.'

'Hang on. I was only joking. But I don't think you are… '

'Well if you spoke Old English – the language of the Anglo-Saxons – you'd know the *here* was no joke. It was their name for the army.'

'Ah! So it's the path used by the army.'

'And quite possibly created by them.'

'Apart from giving them a day out in some nice countryside, what were they doing up here?'

'Presumably they were making sure no undesirables were gathering below the escarpment. A simple system of beacons would enable them to get reinforcements anywhere along the ridge without too much delay. When we're back in the henge I'll tell you more about the Herepath.

'Anyway, we need to make a move. Tell you what though, once you get to know this place a bit better, then sitting up here in the summer watching the sun set is a great experience.'

The gate which leads to the site of Horslip long barrow. You need to walk along the edge of the field past to bush in the centre of the photograph before you can see the unploughed part of the field. And that's all there is to see!

'But then you need to get back down in the dark!'

> 'Well it doesn't get pitch dark until about an hour after sunset. Time it close to the full moon and you might not even need a torch.'

'Think I'd bring one anyway!'

> 'That's more than sensible.'

Grid reference for gate back to track 085711

> 'We're going go through this gate then head directly towards the henge and Silbury Hill down the path going south. It takes us past the site of one of the earthen long barrows, known as Horslip barrow, but there's next to nothing to see now. Look out for a metal gate on your right then follow the field boundary until you get to an area where there's no crop planted.

Grid reference for Horslip barrow 0860 7052

'OK, I can see it. But nothing that looks archaeological.'

> 'No sadly everything was all-but ploughed out. A dig was done just before it disappeared completely.
>
> 'There was no evidence of human remains. Let's get back to the path.'

35

Grid reference for crossroads of paths 089699

'When we get to the cluster of farm buildings we need to cross straight over the other path. if we were going the shortest route back to the henge then we'd turn left. But I'm taking you round the edge of that field. It's not the most level bit of ground around here, but it is a path.

'By the way, if we were to follow this byway to the west, which goes to Yatesbury, in less than half a mile you'd be walking over more or less the place where the remains of a Roman villa were found. But that's a few millennia later than the era we've just be talking about!

Grid reference of Roman villa site: approx. 084700

'Oh, I've just spotted two big stones over there. Shall we head over to them?'

'No, the path doesn't go directly to them. We need to follow the edge of the field and then back track slightly. The stones are known variously as the Longstones, the Devil's Quoits, or as Adam and Eve.'

'Hmmm. Yes one does seem taller and more phallic, and the other, well, more rounded and feminine.'

'I think it's too easy to read too much into how the stones look. And they weren't put up as a pair.'

'Oh? How to you mean?'

'Adam is the last remnant of a "cove" of four stones with a gap to the south-east, while Eve is the sole survivor of the Beckhampton Avenue.'

'The same Beckhampton Avenue that crossed the Winterbourne and then picks up the line of what is now the High Street?

Grid reference for stile from track to stones 088698

'That's it. Turn left at this track and then you'll see a sign where we can go back into the field.

Grid reference for Adam and Eve stones 089693

'There was a really good dig here in the 1990s. They found a small ditched enclosure which was soon back-filled. It may well have been thought of as "archaic" at the time.'

'A deliberately harking back to the good old days?'

'Maybe. The finds gave dates of between 2820 and 2660 BC. And only after that was the cove of stones created – and we think the double stone row or avenue was contemporary with this cove.

'And only a good stone's throw over there was South Street earthen long barrow.'

Grid reference for South Street long barrow SU 0902 6928

'Ah, yes – one of those long barrows that never had chambers or human remains. That would have stood there well before everything else you've described was created or put up.'

'Just so. Interestingly the open side of the cove – of which Adam is the sole survivor – faced towards this barrow. But just to prove that arable farming predated even these early long barrows, there were marks in the soil underneath the barrow which must have been made by a simple plough or ard.'

Grid reference 088692

'OK, so let's get leave this field and get back on the track. We backtrack a little way then dodge around a wooden barrier on the left into an open area of grass.'

Grid reference for Beckhampton Road earthen long barrow 087691

'Why's someone dumped a big load of soil and turf over there?'

'That "load of soil" might look a bit untidy but it's one of the best surviving examples of an earthen long barrow. It's something like how the South Street long barrow would have looked. What we can't see clearly now is the ditches that would have run along each side.'

'So if these never had any sort of burials, what were they for?'

'An exceedingly good question for which archaeologists struggle to come with even a good guess! All we can say is that they would have looked rather like the thatch-roofed wooden houses which early Neolithic people lived in on the Continent. From the size it would seem a whole kin-group, not just a single family, lived in the same house.'

'I've seen those sort of communal houses in TV programmes about Indonesia.'

'And other parts of the world. For fairly obvious reasons timber and thatch houses fall down – or perhaps burn down – fairly regularly. What's really curious is that there's no evidence of them building such big houses in southern Britain, only from further north and in Ireland. But these earthen mounds seem to be monuments to those "idealised" houses.'

'You mean they're based on memories of ancestral houses?'

'Perhaps. If so, they are monuments to those memories. And they do what monuments do best – they survive.'

'Well this one's done that all right – how long has it been standing?

'Five and a half thousand years or near enough.'

'And the one at South Street, although it's gone now, presumably only disappeared in the last few centuries?'

'Indeed. So causewayed camps and long barrows are both the oldest examples of people modifying the landscape, and simultaneously the oldest examples of building monuments.'

'I can't really see a difference... '

'I suppose you're right. What I'm trying to get at is the difference between digging a ditch for practical reasons –

and which may well be filled in again after a short period – and digging a ditch to make a bank or mound which you want to still be there long after you're dead.'

'OK, yes. Though I don't suppose that anyone in the early Neolithic thought that their mounds would be still be around over a hundred generations later.'

'Yes. Five thousand years is difficult to get a handle on. But when you say 100 to 150 generations – though it all depends how old people are when they have children – it shrinks to something that I feel I can *almost* get my head around.'

'For all I know I may be a distant descendant of one of those people.'

'Me too. Indeed anyone who's surname – like mine, Trubshaw – which shows that at least the male line goes back to Anglo-Saxon times is more than likely to have a little bit of prehistoric blood in their veins. It would take much less than a hundred generations for everyone born and bred in England to be ever so slightly related to everyone else, no matter how many phases of immigration there may have been over the millennia.'

'Anyway, let's head down towards the main road – head for those slightly ornate gates to the south then turn left to the roundabout.'

Grid reference 088690

'Oh, it all seems a bit busy with traffic here… '

'Well this is where the road from Devizes to Swindon crosses the A4. That way goes to Calne and the opposite way to Marlborough. And to be honest, I think it was a fairly busy place back in the early Neolithic and even the Mesolithic.'

'Why's that?'

'Remember me saying about how people probably came to here along the Kennet, and up the Avon from Hampshire and from the Bristol Avon? Well the most sensible routes to take from either of the Avons would bring you along the dry valley which runs towards Bishops Cannings and Devizes.'

'And it's along that valley this road to Devizes runs… '

'Exactly. There are quite a lot of Bronze Age barrows still visible, most of which were hurriedly dug by eighteenth and nineteenth century antiquarians. So far rather too little attention has been given to the Neolithic sites and monuments along here.

'Anyway enough of all this talking. Do you fancy a pint and some food? The Waggon and Horses is just a couple of hundred yards along the A4.'

Grid reference for Waggon and Horses 089691

After some refreshments

'Now we can get to Silbury Hill and West Kennett long barrow from here. But it means walking along the road for about five hundred yards.'

'Is there a pavement?'

'No. It means walking facing the oncoming traffic and stepping onto the verge when vehicles are approaching. The road's fairly wide and as it's not rush hour there won't been too many cars and lorries.'

'Sounds a bit hairy to me. Is there another option?'

'Well we can walk back the way we came to the track by the Adam and Eve stones, and then through Avebury Trusloe to Avebury itself. There's not a lot of archaeology but it's an easy stoll over level ground.'

'That sounds better to me. I think we'll take that option.'

'OK. If you check on the OS map you'll see there's a track which runs from just east of the roundabout back towards the Adam and Eve stones.'

Turn right at the track near Adam and Eve. Go past the houses in Avebury Trusloe. At the crossroads go straight over into Frog Lane, then turn left at the end (grid reference 095696), following the signs for the footpath. Once across the field turn right. You will then cross the line of the Beckhampton Avenue (grid reference 096698), although there is nothing to see. Then right again onto a tarmac footpath. Follow around the bend and you will arrive at the bridge over the Winterbourne where you started out (grid reference 097699).

ſєcond walk

This walk is just over mile but, allowing time for looking, will take about an hour.

The starting point is in Avebury High Street by the end of the main path from the visitors' car park (grid reference 101699).

'Hi Simon! We're back at the same place on the High Street where we started the last walk. But this time we're just going to walk around the henge itself. Let's just step inside this gate.'

'So, let me get this right, the henge and the stone circle are built after the causewayed enclosures and long barrows we were looking at on the first walk.'

'Yes. Although to be pedantic you should have said stone circles not stone circle, as there's three of them.'

'I can only see part of one from here… '

'Patience, patience! All will be revealed, as the saying goes.

'Frustratingly most of the archaeology done here was done before the days when there were clever techniques for trying to get dating evidence. So we've still only got a rough idea of when things were built. Although, as always, ideas of dates have changed dramatically, the best guess is that the henge ditch and bank dates from between about 2,800 and 2,600 BC – and current thinking is that most likely around 2,600.

'The outer circle – the one we can see part of here – probably wasn't built before the ditch was dug as all the stones were put in place from the inside rather than the ditch side. So that might be about a century later. But perhaps some of the big stones near the centre of the henge were here before – I'll talk about that when we get to the Cove.'

'But there is some evidence of the stones being used before they were put up. Step up to this first stone.'

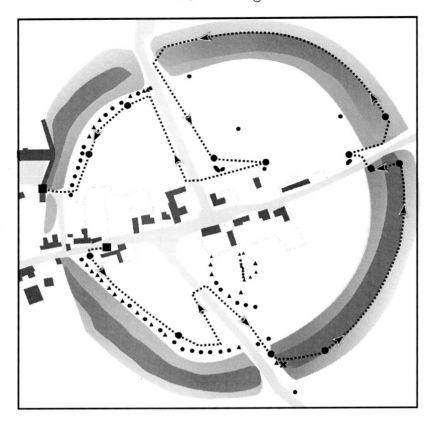

'It's looks like it's been broken up and put back together.'

'Indeed it has. I'll talk about all that in a moment. For a start off run your fingers over just about any part of the surface.'

'Oh, it's a bit like sandpaper.'

'Now run them over this area here… '

'Oh, that's much smoother. But I can barely see any difference. Is there something different about this part of the stone?'

'No. What's different is that early Neolithic people used the stone to polish their stone axes. This type of sandstone – known as sarsen – is both slightly rough and very hard, so it makes a good polishing stone. But to get a polish you also need to lubricate with a little bit of water. So that means this stone was used for polishing *before* it was stood up.'

A polished axe (in replica shaft) on display in the Alexander Keiller Museum. (Photograph reproduced by permission of the Alexander Keiller Museum.)

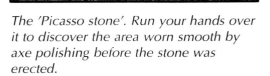

The 'Picasso stone'. Run your hands over it to discover the area worn smooth by axe polishing before the stone was erected.

'Else the water would have just run off. Yes, I can see that if this stone was lying down the smooth area would form a depression. So this is unique?'

'Unusual, but not unique. There's a similar stone in the Avenue, and another inside West Kennett long barrow.'

'Which means it must have been used for polishing before the long barrow was built. And yet you said the long barrows are early... '

'Yes! That one's really interesting as it is one of the few polishing stones which can be dated as really early. We mostly just have to assume the others are about the same age.'

'Must have taken ages to get a good polish on a stone axe. Presumably it made them better for chopping down trees.'

'Well, for a start off an axe is just as useful for butchering animal carcasses as chopping down trees, and maybe we should think of them as a bit like a heavy-duty Swiss army knife which was used for a whole variety of tasks. But, no, the polishing does not seem to make them work any better. So far as well can tell all the effort spent polishing them was simply to make them look better.'

'So it was about looking cool?'

'Almost certainly. Especially when you bear in mind that the stone used for these polished axes often wasn't just any old stone that would do the job. It had to come from some very special outcrops. Many of the axes found throughout the British Isles – including around here – came from an inaccessible part of a scree slope in the Lake District. Yet the same type of stone is found in plenty of places that are easier to get to.'

'It's as if the place where they took the stone had some sort of magical significance.'

'Well, I think we can go as far as to say it must have been a place that had some good myths and legends associated with it. And I'll be showing you a few of those on the next walk too.

'Anyway, the person who put this stone back together was Alexander Keiller. He is also responsible for these concrete markers.'

'Presumably that's where more stones once stood. Where did they go?'

'Indeed they mark the socket holes of now-lost stones. They were broken up, probably to build the houses and boundary walls you see in the High Street.'

'Too good a building material to waste, then.'

Left: *The tools of a tailor or a barber? The early fourteenth century scissors and coins found with the skeleton of the so-called 'barber-surgeon'.*
(Photograph reproduced by permission of the Alexander Keiller Museum.)

Main photograph: *The 'Barber Surgeon' stone.*

'Well, they do make useful building stone. But they are too hard to be easily used. Indeed it was only in about the sixteenth century that people worked out how to break them up – it involves lighting a fire underneath them, pouring water on the hot stone where you want it to split, then hitting it with a sledgehammer. Before that if they wanted a stone out the way they just dug a hole and buried it. Which is why Keiller was able to re-erect the stones you can see over towards the south entrance to the henge.'

'You mean they haven't always stood upright?'

'Only a very few. We know that one of them was buried in the early fourteenth century as a man's skeleton was buried almost beneath the stone.'

'He was squashed when it toppled?'

'Well the skeleton shows no evidence of crushing so he might have been dead before he was buried there.'

'Why not in the churchyard?'

'Who knows. Perhaps he was murdered – although there were coins in his purse so he wasn't robbed. Maybe he was some sort of outsider who the locals didn't like enough to want buried among them. Interestingly he was buried with a pair of scissors and some other implements. Scissors were very rare back them – most people used shears. The scissors and coins and other artefacts found with him are on show in the museum here. Keiller called him a "barber surgeon" but it's just as likely he was a tailor.'

'Either way he's not likely to be someone who lived here. Not enough people to keep a surgeon or even a tailor in business.'

'Indeed.'

'When did Keiller dig up the stones and put them up?'

'This was in the 1930s, after he'd finished excavating on Windmill Hill. It was a major operation. He'd have carried on if it wasn't for the Second World War. Instead we have

You think the ditch is deep now – that's how deep it originally was. A photograph taken during Harold St George Gray's excavations in 1922. (Photograph reproduced by permission of the Alexander Keiller Museum.)

47

about half the henge re-erected by Keiller and about half more-or-less as he found it, which makes for an interesting comparison.

'Did he only find and reinstate the stones?'

'Pretty much. There'd been a major excavation here in the ditch of the south-west sector about twenty years earlier. That showed that they were originally three times the depth than what you can see now, with sides that were nearer to being vertical.'

'*Three times deeper?* Strewth, they're deep enough now. And no JCBs to dig them out back then.'

'No. All hacked out of solid chalk with pick axes and rakes made from antlers. Plus no doubt a great many wicker baskets and ladders made from notched logs, none of which have survived.'

'It's an amazing amount of work. Lots of people were up here for a long time.'

'And, think about it. You could only start building monuments on this sort of scale once you've got farming underway. You could never have a significant number of hunter-gathering type people together in the same place for very long as they would very quickly run out of things to eat. You need to bring, or at the very least store, lots of food *before* you can take on building monuments like this.'

'Yes, I remember what you were saying earlier about the three aspects that change from the Mesolithic to the Neolithic – farming, pottery and monuments.

'And yet Mesolithic people had been coming up here. No definite evidence here in the henge but plenty just a few hundred yards away.

'What exactly is a "henge"? I think of Stonehenge but this really isn't much like that… '

'Well Stonehenge gave its name to all the other henges but really it has little else in common.'

'Well, apart from the stones!'

'No, not even that! There are plenty of henges without any evidence of stones. They may have had timber posts… '

'Ah, like Woodhenge, near Stonehenge.'

Stonehenge. The world's most famous 'henge' – except it isn't a typical henge...

'And others. But some henges may never have had stones or posts. To an archaeologist the word "henge" simply means a ditch with a bank on the *outside*."

'But isn't that the same as some sort of fortification?'

'Not at all! If you were trying to keep somebody out you would put the ditch on the *inside*, not the outside.'

'So if henges really aren't about defence, what are they for?'

'Another of your good questions. There was a time when archaeologists couldn't recognise a practical use for something from the past they simply said it was for "rituals". Frankly "ritual" became a term which covered a lot of lazy thinking. That's no longer the case. But with henges there is plenty of other evidence that we really should think of them as places for rituals.'

'Rituals in which you needed to keep something in? What were you saying before about cattle – I can think that these henges would make excellent bull rings. If a ton or more of prime steak is heading straight toward you, head down and snorting, you can just nip behind a few tons of sarsen and he'll hit that instead.'

'Simon, sometimes your imagination gets the better of you! Though there is plenty of evidence from the Neolithic for ritual sacrifice of cattle. But that falls short of being evidence for bull fighting!;

'So what do you think was being kept in?'

'Maybe souls! Look carefully at these stones. Some of them look a bit like faces. If you come back at different times of day, when the sun lights them up from different directions, then different faces appear. The best examples are the other side of the henge. Wander around at dawn and all sorts of faces seem to be looking back at you. Come back a few hours later and it's hard to make them out at all...

'Think how we have very clear walls about boundaries around churchyards and cemeteries, with lych gates and the like at entrances. We are still keen that the dead "stay in their place". Yet even so recently as a couple of hundred years ago, throughout Britain and Europe there was still a great fear of the "restless dead".

'Ghosts and revenants and all that?'

'Yes, those fears fuelled a lot of nineteenth century Gothick novels and the like. And those novels provided the storylines for a whole industry of horror movies – with a few resurrected Egyptian mummies and Caribbean zombies thrown in for good measure. But even taking away the more lurid of these ideas, would you want the souls of the dead to start wandering around? No, trapping them in very large stones and put a large ditch and bank around them seems a very sensible thing too do!'

'Have archaeologists found any evidence of these souls?'

'You're not taking my idea very seriously are you, Simon? No, of course it is only an idea. But one reason why I think I might be about right is that in the Iron Age the whole of the henge area seems to have been a "taboo" place.'

'Did someone find a 'Keep Out – Dangerous spirits within' notice from the Iron Age then Bob?'

'No. They've found nothing.'

One of the many 'simulacra' – natural shapes in the stones which look like faces – to be found on the sarsens of Avebury henge. Most are only clearly visible in bright sunlight – and at certain times of day.

'Eh?'

'And in this case finding nothing is really quite interesting!'

'You've lost me... '

'I know. We know Iron Age people were all around here as there's plenty of Iron Age hill forts within a few miles of here – Barbury and Liddington Castle to the north-east, Oldbury just over there to the west and Rybury a bit further away to the south-west. But no real evidence of Iron Age activity has been found in or near the henge.'

'Is that because archaeologists have not looked in the right places?'

'Unlikely. There's been enough deliberate "looking" together with chance finds for the absence to be real.'

'So absence of evidence is, for once, evidence of absence... '

'Just so. And the only reasonable explanation is that the Iron Age people were too afraid to come here.'

'But they were famous for their warriors and heroes.'

'So it must have been a fairly powerful myth that kept them away.'

'Presumably so. Hang on – hasn't there been an archaeologist on the TV in recent years saying that Stonehenge is a place of the dead while Durrington Walls, up the road, is a place of the living?'

'Indeed. That's Mike Parker Pearson. If he's right – and I'm inclined to broadly agree, although I suspect Neolithic peoples' thinking was a bit more complex – then by the Iron Age the ideas had evolved into this being a "dead zone".

'But there are all sorts of tantalising bits of evidence which suggest that ideas about souls go back well before the Neolithic, along with some suggestions that there was a belief in reincarnation.

'So the souls in these stones are not so much trapped as waiting for the chance to be reborn?'

'Well, that's certainly consistent with what I'm saying. I wonder if archaeologists will ever be able to prove your suggestion?'

'Now you're the one being facetious!'

'The problem is that everyone has their own idea of what this place was about. Mostly the ideas just reflect modern day assumptions and beliefs. But the way we today can come up with so many different ideas is probably a clue that, over the many generations it was used in prehistory, there were lots of different notions too, as people's ideas changed.'

'That would be a bit like the way, say, a cathedral or parish church has been used for about a thousand years, but there were big changes at the Reformation, various changes in the eighteenth century, and then some quite radical rethinks about liturgy in the first half of the nineteenth.'

'And then in the last fifty years some churches have gone for something different again – the sort of style of worship that got nicknamed "happy clappy".'

'So you're saying that prehistoric people may have changed this as often?'

'Maybe more often if there was not a deeply traditional hierarchy like the Church of England synod controlling the pace of change.'

One of the many sarsens with holes left by tree and plant roots about thirty million years ago.,

'So perhaps we shouldn't think of the past as doing one thing for most of the time. Perhaps it was more about changes and even different people doing different things more-or-less at the same time?'

> 'That seems the most sensible approach, though it makes it incredibly difficult to say anything very specific about what those ideas might have been, least of all at any one time or place.'

'Anyway, while we've been talking I've noticed that with all these sarsens the bumpier side is towards the ditch and the smoother side faces inwards. Was that because they were smoothed off?'

> 'No, unlike the sarsens used at Stonehenge – which were squared off – none of the stones in the Avebury henge have any signs of being worked. The holes and other undulations are fossilised remains of tree and plants. Or, more accurately, the holes left by the roots.'

53

Looking to the south entrance from inside the south circle.

'Surely the plants couldn't bore holes into such hard stone... '

'No. They were living in the sand roughly thirty million years ago, before it all turned to stone. The whole of this area was covered in a shallow depth of sand, sitting on top of the chalk. It hardened and, for a long time after, protected the chalk from erosion. But gradually the chalk dissolved away and without any support the hard sandstone just steadily broke up. With the help of one or more of the ice ages it moved around a little bit – certainly more ended up in valleys than elsewhere. It is said that until the seventeenth century it was possible to get all the way across the Marlborough Downs by jumping from one sarsen to another.'

'But there's hardly any up there now!'

'Indeed, just some on Fyfield Down – it's just past the Ridgeway on the skyline over there – and another small area over at Lockeridge. But most of it was broken up for building and road stone.'

'But it did mean that when they wanted to make this stone circle they didn't have to go too far to find suitable stones.'

'Indeed. And it might be the other way about – one of the reasons they created the henge was because of the stones.

'Now we've almost got to the road we'll need to follow the fence back to the gate. Don't take too much interest in the way the ditch and bank appears near this side of the road. It's because the southern entrance and the road were moved at the end of the eighteenth century.'

'Was there a southern entrance before?'

'Yes, it's just that it was a few yards over there. All the part of the bank on the opposite side of the road, where the beech trees are growing, wasn't there before. But a similar amount of bank was standing on this side. And they created this bank parallel to the road as part of the change.'

'Why did they move it?'

'It doesn't seem that necessary now but it was to straighten up the route into the lane alongside the Avenue, so the coaches didn't have to do a sharp 'S'-bend.

'Anyway, follow the fence towards the gate where it's safer to cross the road.'

'Remember I said that there were really three stone circles here once? The outer one we've seen part of. These big stones are what is left of the southern circle. Follow the curve around and you'll see it passes through where those buildings are now.'

'What about the little stones in the middle? They're a circle too!'

'Almost. But one side of the circle is straight, so they're more like a 'D'. And not only are they smaller than the other surviving stones but they're a much redder colour too.'

'Why?'

'We don't know but presumably it was important to the people who put them up. All we really know about this D-shaped area is that the tallest stone at Avebury was once in the middle.'

'Ah! I can see a different shape concrete marker... '

'That's where it stood. It had already fallen and broken by the eighteenth century. William Stukeley, who did a drawing of it, measured it as being over twenty feet long, so it stood

The Obelisk stone drawn in 1723 by William Stukeley. Within a few years it had been broken up. The south entrance and Waden Hill are in the distance.

perhaps fifteen or more feet tall. He called it the Obelisk. But not long after he drew it the remains were broken up.

'Turn round and look between those two big stones in front of the beech trees. Imagine the beech trees and that part of the bank weren't there.'

'I'd be looking straight at the southern entrance through the ditch.'

'Just so. And as these are the biggest pair of stones surviving they make an impressive entrance. The other entrances seem also once to have had pairs of impressive stones too – although at the northern entrance only one survives, but it is still standing. At the eastern entrance again there's only one and that's now lying down.

'Walk between the stones.'

'There's like a seat on this one to the west.'

'Indeed it is popularly known as the Devils' Chair. Sit in it and look up.

'Oh! There's a hole in the stone all the way to the sky!

'Rather interesting, eh? And I don't think it's in the least bit accidental.'

The 'Chair Stone' and its companion either side of the original southern entrance.

'No – someone sitting here could have a ritual libation poured over them from up there.'

> 'And you're facing one of the main entrances – bear in mind what I was saying a few moments ago about the entrance originally being where the beech trees now are – with the end of the West Kennett Avenue just over there. I could take you across the road and up to the Avenue, but it would make more sense if we come down the Avenue towards the henge after we've been to Silbury Hill.'

If you prefer to walk up the Avenue as part of this walk then see pages 122 to 130 for further information.

'OK. You think the Avenue was an approach to the henge rather than a way from it then?'

> 'Very much so. You'll see why when we walk along it.
>
> 'Before we wander off, do you see that different-shaped concrete marker at the edge of the ditch?'

'What, the round one?'

The round concrete marker near the southern entrance marks the site of a post hole much bigger in diameter than the concrete post.

'That's it.

'Is that another marker for a lost stone?'

'No, all the missing stones are marked by rectangular markers. That one marks where a wooden post nearly a yard across once stood.'

'That's massive! Was it tall as well?'

'Who knows, but presumably so.'

'How old was the tree?'

'Sadly none of the wood survived and there is no way to date it. Frankly it could be anything from a few hundred years old to one of the original features before the henge was built.'

'Why do you think it could be so old?'

'Well, if there were two of them – and if there ever were the second one would have been lost when they moved the road – then it would be like the massive post holes found in the car park near Stonehenge. And those were dated to the Mesolithic.'

'So it could, as you say, have been here long before the henge.

A cross-section of the earlier bank photographed when the henge bank was excavated in 1969 prior to the building of a new school. (Photograph reproduced by permission of the Alexander Keiller Museum.)

Shame no one is likely to find out for certain. You know what I think it was?'

    'Go on... '

'I think there was only ever one hole and in it was an upturned tree, with the roots in the air – like the Seahenge they found on the Norfolk coast a few years back.'

    'Yes, a few other people have thought that too. Seahenge was Neolithic rather than Mesolithic but, if there is any truth in the idea, then such a wooden monument presumably predates the henge as we know it.

    'Actually it's about here that early archaeologists got an insight into an earlier henge bank. When they put a trench through the bank as it is now, they found a small bank – only a couple of yards across and about a yard high. There was evidence that turf had grown on the top but sometime after, and no knows how long that was, this bank was buried by the bank you see now.'

'Did they find a ditch too?'

'No, but there almost certainly was one. It's just that the later ditch would have removed any evidence for the earlier one.

'Of course, silly me.'

'But it does suggest that the design for the henge was laid out before they went to all the trouble of digging these huge ditches.'

'A trial run?'

'Not really. The original ditches would have been almost as big as those on Windmill Hill, so it was certainly a monument in its own right. They would be bigger than the only ditch and bank at Stonehenge. It's more that someone decided they needed to do something that made even more of a statement.

'Let's walk up these steps and take a look at the henge from up on the bank.'

See photograph on page 2.

'This is where I feel I can begin to understand the layout of the place. And I see now why you think Windmill Hill is so important to understanding the henge. If we think of this henge bank as forming an amphitheatre around the stones then, at least from this side of the bank, then Windmill Hill provides the "backdrop". OK, the trees near the High Street partly block the view nowadays, but once you realise Windmill Hill's there, it really is difficult to ignore it.

'It's very different being up there from being down here with the stones. When you're on the ground it's more tricky because of the houses and so on. How old are the houses?

'Nothing that seems to go back before the sixteenth century. Indeed, there's nothing to suggest people were living in the henge much before the twelfth century. The early settlement was outside the henge bank – I'll show you more about that on our next walk.

'Presumably the first road through the middle was the east-west one which is now Green Street and the High Street, with the Devizes to Swindon road coming later after buildings had appeared, as this does a dog-leg rather than neatly cross over. By the time this north-south route is in use

The beech trees by the eastern entrance to the henge.

coaches had become an increasingly important way of getting about, so people would have set up in business as pubs and inns.'

'Just like the Red Lion today.'

'Remember that there were more cottages and farm buildings in the middle of the henge until the 1950s when the National Trust knocked down some that were deemed unfit for living in by the standards of the time.'

'Apart from the southern circle there aren't as many stones in the outer circle as over there where we've just been.'

'That's because Keiller's work stopped in 1939 with the outbreak of the war. He never got to excavate and re-erect the stones in the outer circle in this part of the henge.'

'Are the stones still there, buried?'

'Some are, some have been broken up and lost.'

'How can you be so sure?'

'There have been some surveys over the years. The earliest such survey was in 1885 by Reverend A.C. Smith – and it was surprisingly accurate! Smith got his workmen to poke an iron rod into the ground and seeing if it hit anything large. Modern surveys use geophysics such as resistivity and subtle variations in magnetism and gravity.

'Let's just keep walking to the beech trees at the eastern entrance. Like the ones at the southern entrance they're just over two hundred years old – there is a drawing of these ones in the east dated 1805 and it shows the trees as saplings.'

'The roots are really interesting. And without them presumably there would have been much more erosion.'

'Indeed. Take it steady as you drop down to the gate.'

'Now do watch out for the traffic as you cross – this used to be the main road from London to Bath.'

'You're joking! It's just a farm track. Look, the OS map shows it more or less peters out into a bridleway up to the Ridgeway.'

'I'm not joking. The modern A4 follows a turnpike road which was built as a detour around the fairly steep slope up to the Ridgeway. It must have been a nightmare to get coaches down it, let alone up it.'

'When was this road made then?'

'Well, if you look at the map again you'll see it's the continuation of the Herepath that we saw from the top of Windmill Hill.'

'Ah, so the Anglo-Saxon army created it.'

'Possibly. At the very least they used a route that was there before. We'll come out along this road and follow in their footsteps on our next walk.

If you want to skip the rest of the henge and set off on the Third Walk then turn to page 74.

'Now we're through the gate just walk over to this fallen stone.'

'It's another big one – that's because it was near an entrance, right?'

'Yes that seems to be the case. Presumably there was another big one across the lane but that's long gone. Look

The now-recumbent stone near the eastern entrance. It almost certainly once stood upright on the flat surface nearest to the camera.

carefully at the western side and you can see that it has a flat base which would have made it fairly easy to get it to stand up.

'Now let's climb back up to the top of the henge bank again.'

'This part of the henge bank is much more undulating. Is this also erosion?'

'Good question! Probably. But really we have no idea whether the banks were built with a level top.'

'But what we were walking on was fairly level. And the south-west quadrant where we started was also fairly level.'

'And so too is the fourth quadrant, which we'll get to last. But they are level because archaeologists "tidied them up". This quadrant of henge bank has not been tidied up, though some parts have been dug into by farmers over the centuries,

as with this gap here. Because no one knows how "original" the undulations are then this part of the henge bank is the most vulnerable to wear caused by visitors' feet. When the ground's dry there's not much of a problem but the National Trust close it off when the weather turns wet.'

'There's even fewer stones in this sector than the previous one. But there's two really huge ones over there. But they're not near an entrance.'

'Indeed. Those two are the surviving part of what is know as the Cove.'

'There were more?'

'Well, one more. Interestingly, bearing in mind your thoughts about this being a bull ring, when the three stones still stood they would have looked a bit like two horns either side of a head. And there are plenty of temples and other sacred sites around the Mediterranean where just than same configuration is often intentional.

'Remember what you said about Windmill Hill being the backdrop from the south side of the bank. What's the backdrop now?'

'Well, that must be Waden Hill. Yes, again, it seems to dominate the henge itself. Once you notice it you can't ignore it, just the same way that Windmill Hill can't be ignored from the south.

'Now we've almost got the road and before we drop down into the henge itself again, just look across the road.'
'It's another of the large entrance stones'.

'Yes that one's known as the Swindon Stone or the Diamond Stone.'
'Ah, ha, yes it does seem to be standing on one corner.'

'We'll walk up to it a few minutes. But bear in mind what I said about these portal stones coming in pairs... '
'Ah, so you're saying there was another one like it this side of the road too.'

'The earliest of the antiquarians mention what might have been a pillar-like stone. But it had gone by the time Stukeley got here. Based on the distance between the stones at the southern entrance I suspect the second one was just this side of the road.'
'I can see a stone here to the east from the outer circle. But what are all these smaller stones? They look like a low wall.'

'Yes, they are from a fairly modern field boundary. You can see a low mound running around just inside the ditch. That's where a stone wall or hedge ran all the way round this part. There were also several hedges and walls breaking up this sector into fields. They all went in the 1930s.

'Anyway, let's make our way over to the Cove.'
'It really is big when you get close up.'

'And so far as we can tell the ground surface was nearly two feet lower when the stones were put up. Until the 1950s there were farm buildings and cottages nearby.

This really big one is estimated at about a hundred tons in weight. It's the biggest of all the stones that have survived in the henge. And I think it always was the biggest.'
'So they must have practised on the smaller ones first before getting the knack of moving this one.'

'Well, although we don't know exactly when any of the other stones were put up, when there a serious archaeological dig around both of these stones in the mid-

A photograph of the Cove taken in the nineteenth century.
The adjoining buildings were demolished in the late 1950s.
(Photograph reproduced by permission of the Alexander Keiller
Museum.)

1990s a new dating technique was used which suggests this stone was put up between 3,400 and 2,800 BC. Which would mean it is likely to be among the first. It's also a close match to the early phases of the ditch at Stonehenge, although before any of the stones there.'

'So the rest of the henge and the stones circles were laid out *around* this?'

'If it is true, then I think all three of the Cove stones – don't forget the missing one – were about contemporary. But the location of the Cove within the henge is significant. Remember I said about the henge being a bit like an upturned saucer? It's tricky to make out because of the houses – but the Cove is on the highest part of that dome. And if you look over between the pub and the antique shop you can just see the top of Silbury Hill over the henge bank.

This is the only place inside the henge where you can do that.'

'But I thought Silbury wasn't built till after the henge was finished...'

'That's true. But the henge certainly wasn't out of use when Silbury Hill was built.

'If the opening to the Cove – the side where there never was a fourth stone – is to the north-east it looks towards the midsummer sunrise then?'

'No. None of the stones at Avebury make an obvious alignment with the sun or the moon.'

'Come on, with this many stones – and the positions of most of the missing ones known from surveys – surely there are loads of alignments?'

'Well having that many stones does mean that you could line up just about anything with anything. But even that doesn't work very well. There is a stone in the Avenue which is "turned round" to face the midsummer sunrise. Once you're aware of it that stands out – we'll take a look on our next walk. But there's nothing "obvious" which links the henge to the sun, or the moon. But the direction in which this Cove faces is where one of the brightest stars in the sky Deneb was rising around five thousand years ago.'

'Can't say I've taken much interest in Deneb myself.'

'It's in the constellation Cygnus – meaning "the swan" of course – which looks a bit like a swan head-down in the sky or a Christian cross. The constellation is in the Milky Way, so even if the Milky Way can't been seen clearly, Deneb can still be seen.'

'Yes, there's so much light pollution these days that even on a very clear night it's often hard to see the Milky Way.'

'Interestingly, around here there are times when it can be seen. Although with Swindon to the north of here then sadly the rising of Deneb is lost in the light pollution from there.'

'So you think the Cove is about swans not bulls then?'

'I'm not excluding the link with bulls. But I do think that there's a connection between swans and souls. It may even go back well into the Mesolithic. It's too complicated to explain here – you'll have to read my book *Singing Up the Country*! Suffice to say that the souls of the deceased may have been thought to travel on the backs of swans.

'A bit like folklore would have us believe that babies are brought by storks.'

'Well, if you made that the *soul* of the baby which was delivered by such birds then it all seems very similar.

'Anyway, enough speculation, let's get back to being here at the Cove. Turn so your back is against this main stone. Where are you facing?'

'Well, as the opposite way is north-east, obviously it's south-west...'

'Well, that's true enough. But I didn't mean it like that. If we set off walking that way where would we get to?'

'That's tricky – there's not only the pub in the way but also a hill. Pass me the map please...

'Ah ha! If the little hill wasn't in the way we'd be look straight down the dry valley you keep talking about – the one from Beckhampton to Devizes. In other words, the route people coming up from the valleys of the two different River Avons would be using.'

'And maybe they thought the souls of the recently-deceased came the same way, perhaps stopping within the henge if they were to be reborn, perhaps keeping on going all the way to the "swan in the sky", the constellation Cygnus. "North, beyond the north wind" as Scandinavian folklore says about the land of the dead. Only in this case more like north-east.

'So people would see real swans and think that they were carrying souls?'

'Maybe. And which way do you think swans migrate each year?'

'I don't know for certain but a quick guess is that they'd be coming up the river valleys... '

'Indeed. And they go north in early November, between the time of the Christian feasts of All Souls and Martinmass.'

'Hang on, Martinmass is traditionally when people held goose fairs. I can't help think that geese and swans are remarkably similar in appearance.'

'Me too. Anyway, now we're both getting carried away with these ideas. I just want you to think how this Cove would have looked when then the third stone still stood. And then think how our voices would have *sounded* if we were standing here inside the three.'

'Well, it's obvious there would have been some good echoes. Listen *[Claps hands steadily]* Even clapping between these two stones gets an interesting response.'

'Yes, the stones would help the sound carry. They would also stop anyone outside the Cove from hearing at all well. While the sound would carry to anyone towards the north-east.'

'Well I guess it's just what would happen no matter which way it faced.'

'Which way does the horseshoe of blue stones at Stonehenge face?'

'Is this some sort of test? I don't know. But with that look in your eye I'm going to guess. North-east?'

'Right first time. And the way the stones in the Stonehenge horseshoe reflect sound creates even more interesting multiple echoes.'

'So you think this was where they got together to do a spot of shamanic drumming and all that, five thousand years before modern day pagans?'

'I'm not so sure there were any drums as such back then. And the word "shamanic" tells us more about the academics who use it – in all sorts of ever-changing ways – than it does about traditional religions. But people could be chanting, clapping – as you just did, beating hardwood sticks together, whirling bull roarers or playing flutes made from bird bones.'

'Hang on, I thought we'd stopped speculating about bulls and swans. Now you're talking about bull roarers and bird bones again.'

'Sorry. Actually we don't know why the simple musical instrument known in English as a "bull roarer" got it's name. We do know that the same instruments are used throughout the world, as far away as Australia, and usually often only for men's initiation rituals and the like. And we don't know

One of the clearest simulacra which have survived – although it is only seen clearly at sunrise.

if the ancient bird bone flutes came from swans. After all bird bones are among the first to break up and be lost.

'Let's move on. But before we head through that gate and cross the road, let's check out what's left of the north circle.'

'Ah yes, when we were at the south circle you said there was a north circle too. Can't say I'd really noticed one.'

'Well that's understandable. All that's standing is this big stone here, that one over there, and a fragment near to it. The one over there is especially interesting. Go over and stand on the south side, and look at it from the side. What do you see?'

'Not a lot. The usual sort of bumps and hollows.'

'True. When you get a chance, come back at sunrise, preferably spring or autumn. Those bumps look for all the world like someone staring at the rising sun. I've nicknamed this stone the "Dawn Watcher". And if you do come back, look around the henge for other faces that can only be seen clearly at dawn. I won't spoil the surprise by telling you where they all are! Suffice to say that the place really seems to be alive.'

'If that's true, and I don't doubt you, then I can see why you think that the Neolithic people thought that these stones where were their relative's souls were residing.'

'OK, enough! It really is time to move on. Back to the gate by the road and then we'll cross over. Take care – the traffic whizzes round the corner to our left.'

'You get a good view of the Swindon Stone walking down this fenced off path.'

'Yes. You get a real sense of it being a "gateway" or portal stone with it being so close to the road. The two stones at the southern entrance might be even bigger but they've lost that sense of the entrance being between them.'

'I can see this is the other sector where Keiller did his stuff. There's more of the concrete markers and all the stones are standing up again.'

'Not only that, he cut down a whole row of trees along the top of the henge bank and then dynamited the tree stumps.'

'You're joking?'

'No, there's a photo to prove it!'

'Then presumably he tidied the bank up to the nice even profile we can see now.'

'That's right. He was quite meticulous at getting the profile right.

'Take a look at the remains of this stone.'

'What, this one that looks like a seat?'

'That's the one. It's all that's left of a much bigger stone that was broken up sometime after the sixteenth century. Keiller only found this part, but it is the base so he put it back. But he wasn't the first to re-erect this particular stone.'

'How do you mean?'

'Well, unusually, there was clear evidence of it having been stood up again in the Bronze Age. Even more unusually there was a fragment of a human skull buried underneath it from that time.'

The remains of the stone which was re-erected in the Bronze Age, with its neighbours.

'So is it unusual because there was only a fragment of the skull or because there was any human bone at all?'

'The latter. While there is evidence of Neolithic burials in the Avenue – and there may well be more, as Keiller did not specifically look for these – very few human remains have been found in the henge. And, although a lot has never been excavated, enough has been done to get a fairly representative look at the ditch, the areas around the stones, and such like.

'Stay on the outside of the stones towards the ditch. This stone is an unusual shape.'

'Yes. I think if I came along here at dusk or even the dark with just a burning torch, I'd easily think this was a larger-than-life human head.

'OK if we go through the gate and down the steps we get to the café. Shall we have something to eat before going around the two museum exhibitions?'

'I definitely need a break before doing even one museum. Why two?'

'Well really it's one museum but the exhibits are in two buildings. The huge thatched barn contains models and

The 'head stone'.

interpretation panels. Most of the actual finds are in the old stables building at the far end of this old farmyard.'

'Isn't that where you said there were skeletons of a goat, pig and dog from Windmill Hill?'

'Yes. And flint tools, pots and other artifacts.'

'Not to be missed!'

'Indeed! They're very much an essential part of trying to get to know these monuments.'

'And after than can we stop at the shop here as well? I seem to remember you saying that they stock some of your other books too.'

Third walk

This walk is about six miles and, allowing time for looking at the sites, will take about three to fours hours.

Grid reference for start 103700

> 'Hi Simon. Are you ready for another longish walk? We need to cross the road near the Red Lion and head off east up Green Street.'

'That's towards the eastern entrance of the henge, right? Didn't you say it was also the old coach route to London and the Anglo-Saxon Herepath?'

> 'Well, what's now both the High Street and Green Street follow the Herepath. But the old coach route came up from the southern entrance and turned along Green Street.

'We'll just follow past the henge bank till we get past a few houses and the farm buildings.'

A few hundred yards later. Grid reference 111133

> 'We're going to take this byway to the right. But the rather deeply rutted route you see going straight on up to the Ridgeway on the skyline is the old coach road. And some of those ruts will have been started by the coaches.'

'I don't envy the drivers – or even the horses. I can see why they wanted to create an easier route.'

> 'Now I'm not intending to go up this byway but if we did we would cross over the Ridgeway and enter Fyfield Down. It's one of the few areas where sarsens still survive in something like their original way. And, even more interesting, there's a small standing stone which marks where three parishes come together. It's probably wasn't put up until the Anglo-Saxon era or even more recently. But right beside it is one of the best examples of a polisher stone – and one that's still lying down as it was used.

'Shall we go there?'

The polisher stone on Fyfield Down. There are several parallel grooves and a flatter area (to the left) created by axe polishing over five thousand years ago.

In the middle distance is the stone erected to mark where three parishes meet.

Visiting these would add over three miles to the walk. If you want to go there the Grid reference is 128716.

'Well it will add well over three miles to our route so that's not really sensible.'

'OK, let's stick to plan!'

'In that case we need to turn off and walk towards those clumps of beech trees. The shape of the hill is especially interesting, especially to place-name reseachers.'

'Why's that?'

'Well there's a long level stretch and then a curve which gets steeper as it drops down. It's been compared to an upturned canoe.'

'Yes, that seems apt.'

'And it's called Overton Hill. The "-ton" at the end means "settlement" so Overton is the settlement near the over. And that's exactly what an over looks like – a hill shaped like an upturned canoe. There a plenty of places called Over or Overton or such like in England and almost all of them have hills that, at least from one direction, look like this one. Only here there are no buildings or even that many trees to

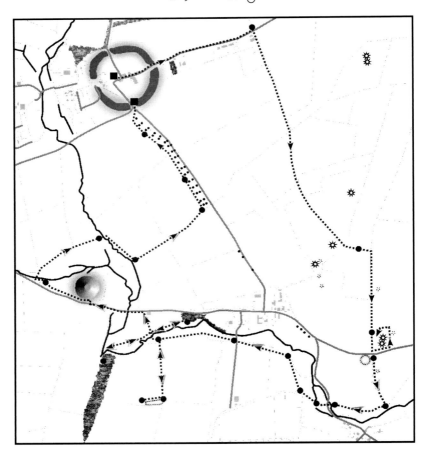

obscure the shape, as there are with many other over places.'

'So an Anglo-Saxon who didn't know the area well would know from a distance that he was walking towards Overton because he could see the over-shaped hill from a distance? Clever!'

'Especially when you consider that the Anglo-Saxons had at least twenty words for different shaped hills – so a "don" wasn't an "over" and a "cliff" wasn't a "shelf", and such like.'

'How many words? That's more words for hills than Eskimos have for snow!'

Overton Hill as seen from near the start of this walk.

> 'Allegedly! For what's worth, we have a "don" over there, even though it's spelt differently now – Waden Hill. Like all "don" hills it has a very rounded top.'

'If an over looks like an upturned canoe, then Waden Hill looks like a beached whale!'

> 'Indeed. But not all "don" hills look quite so much like whales! Anyway look towards the bottom of Waden Hill, near the hedge by the road. As we follow this track you'll begin to make out the stones of the Avenue running just the other side of the road.

'Ah, yes, it's becoming clearer as we keep rising a little bit higher up.'

> 'Now, it's tricky to spot it until you know where it is, but follow you eye from where the stones of the Avenue end – it's where a couple of cars are parked in the little layby – and then follow the hedge running roughly towards up on this side of the road. And towards this end of the hedge there's a small stone sitting on its own.'

Grid reference for Falkner's Circle 110694.

The surviving stone of Falkner's Circle is behind the hedge when viewed from this part of the walk. However the stones of the Avenue are visible between the road and Waden Hill.

'Where? I'm struggling... Ah, yes – got it!'

'That's the only surviving part of what may have been a very small stone circle. It was sketched back in 1810 by an antiquarian from Devizes called Mr Falkner but was destroyed sometime after that. It has been known ever since as Falkner's Circle. But whether it really was a stone circle or just a natural ring of stones, or something half-way in-between – a "man-modified" place rather than a "man-made" one – is all a bit up in the air. In the mid-1990s archaeologists tried to determine what was what but they really didn't get any conclusive evidence. But what they did find, to their surprise, was a lot of Mesolithic flint.'

'So people had been camping there before they were building stone circles and such like?'

'Just so.'

'A bit of a coincidence that.'

'Probably not. The archaeologists suggested that the place was in some way special in the Mesolithic and – through stories and myths – continued to have special significance into the Neolithic. It seems that by the Neolithic there was

All that remains of Falkner's Circle.

already a fairly well-developed sense of "the past", even though that sense was presumably was more genealogical and mythical rather than historical. However, be that as it may, there are a number of places on this side of the dry valley where clusters of Mesolithic flint have been found. It seems to have been a popular place.

'We could follow the edge of the field and take a closer look if you like. If we hadn't planned on going all the way to West Kennett long barrow and Silbury Hill then it's easy to get to the end of the Avenue and follow it back to the henge.'

If you opt for this much shorter walk then information about the Avenue is on pages 122 to 130.

'No? OK, so we'll carry on steadily climbing up to the Ridgeway. I must admit this gentle climb obliquely across the face of the escarpment is much easier than the straight-up ascent we saw from Green Street.'

Grid reference for beech tree clump 117688

'It's interesting seeing these clumps of beech trees from closer up. From down in the henge they appear to be on the skyline. But now we're getting closer it seems that the skyline – which is the Ridgeway – is another two or three hundred yards further on.'

One of the beech tree clumps planted on Bronze Age barrows.
They appear to be on the skyline when seen from this distance.

'Yes. Each clump of trees was planted on and around one or more Bronze Age barrows. Quite clearly these barrows were meant to be seen on the skyline from the henge – and from the Avenue too – and were quite cleverly situated.'

'Yes, very clever. Now I seem to remember the Bronze Age is from just over four thousand years ago to less than three thousand years ago. So these barrows built at any time around then?'

'Most likely the earlier part of that period. It's the same time as they were putting barrows on top of Windmill Hill.'

'Which is easy to see over there… '

'Quite. Although intriguingly while we can see Windmill Hill from here near the barrows, once we get to the Ridgeway it will be almost impossible to see Windmill Hill. Indeed one of the few ways it can be seen is by standing on top of one of the bigger Bronze Age barrows!'

'So the siting may be even clever than I first thought?'

'So it seems. But we don't know how many Bronze Age barrows have been ploughed out and lost. There are several

When standing at the Bronze Age barrows Windmill Hill is visible to the north. Walk just a few yards further towards the Ridgeway and Windmill Hill disappears from view.

groups along the dry valley from Beckhampton to Devizes – and some of these are in the valley bottom, not near the tops of the hills.

Grid reference 119688

'If we just walk a few more yards and turn right onto the Ridgeway we'll soon get to one of the most impressive group of Bronze Age barrows to have survived around here. And as some of them have been excavated by archaeologists then we have a better idea of what as there.'

'Ah, yes, this track is clearly the Ridgeway. Am I right in thinking that over there, to the north, is the Iron Age Hill fort of Barbury Castle? And then it goes on past the famous early Neolithic chamber tomb we know as Waylands Smithy, and Uffington White Horse and the Iron Age hill fort just above it?'

'That's the one!'

'So we're now walking on a path that the people who built the early Neolithic tombs, and the Iron Age hill forts, and what have you all walked!'

'No!'

'What do you mean? They must have come this way?'

'Indeed, I fully agree that people are very likely to have travelled between such places, and following a prominent ridge both offers an easy route and is easy to follow. But there's a slight problem... '

'Go on... How "slight" is this problem?'

'In the Bronze Age there were field boundaries – presumably earth banks with ditches, possibly with stone walls on top – every few hundred yards going straight across all this stretch of the Ridgeway, seemingly for several miles.'

'But there could have been gates to let people and animals pass through.'

'No, the crop mark photographs and detailed surveys simply show unbroken banks. So while people may have been following the ridge in the Neolithic, in the Bronze Age they must have been using a different route to get between the little farms which were spread out among all those fields. From the evidence that we have it seems likely that the route was being used by the Romans, but it's not all that clear when the Ridegway comes into use – or back into use – as a routeway.

'For what's worth, my guess is that there was an earlier route slightly off the summit which went between where the barrows now are.'

'Have the archaeologists found any evidence?'

'So far as I'm aware they've not even looked. But I'm not sure what sort of evidence they could find if they did.'

Grid reference 119683

'Look to our left. What do you see?'

'Rather a lot of Bronze Age barrows.'

'Good enough answer. The group is known as Seven Barrows, but there are ten recognisable ones now and maybe originally more.'

Seven Barrows seen from the Ridgeway.

'So a bit of a misnomer! Who couldn't count?'

'There are plenty of groups of barrows around England known as Seven Barrows but, as with these, usually there are clearly more than seven. It seems that seven was like a "magic number" that almost meant the same as "many". Folklore – and the popular names given to prehistoric monuments and such like are good examples of folklore – is like that. Things aren't always literal, there is an element of metaphor and allusion.

'However, not that you were to know, more interestingly the archaeological digs have shown that not all of them are Bronze Age – some of the now-lost ones are Roman. And there's also one of the best-preserved stretches of Roman road in Wiltshire. Not to mention a good number of the burials in and around the barrows turned out to be Anglo-Saxon.'

'I didn't know the Romans built barrows.'

'They didn't do it very often, so these ones here were rather special. Actually they were drum-shaped tombs rather than mounded barrows. Sadly there's almost nothing left to see now.'

Grid reference 119681

'Keep on walking down the track for a while till we get to the little gate. Head for the impressive-looking one straight ahead. This one is Bronze Age. Before you start walking up it, just take a look over your left shoulder to the north-west. What can you see? Do you recognise any prehistoric sites?'

'Can't see a lot – the henge is hidden by the slope and the trees.'

'OK, fair enough. Now walk up to the top of this barrow. How look again... '

'Hey, isn't that Windmill Hill over there – with all the barrows like this one on the top?'

'Well spotted! It's tricky to make out. Interesting that you have to stand on this barrow before you can see them though, isn't it?'

''Just a little too interesting, I'd say.'

Grid reference 119683

'Anyway keep walking this way. There's a rather slight rise in the ground, then a flat bit, then another slight rise.'

'Yes, got the first one... And here's the second. But it doesn't seem to be a circular feature like the barrows. In fact, I can just make out a pair of very shallow long mounds or banks in the grass.'

'Well I did say one of the best preserved bits of Roman road was up here!'

'So these two shallow mounds are at the sides of a Roman road? Well, if this is a well-preserved Roman road it doesn't say much for the state of the less well-preserved Roman roads!'

'That's true. The two shallow banks would of course have been more substantial, with ditches. There were known in Latin as *fossa*.'

'Ah ha – would I be right in thinking that's how the Fosse Way from Cirencester to Lincoln gets its name?'

'You would. And this road is another long-distance main route.'

'London to Bath I guess – the precursor to the A4 which is just over there. Which means that, if you're right about the Ridgeway also being another Roman route, then we're standing at a Roman crossroads.

'Well spotted! Now if you were an important Roman person you wanted your tomb to be seen by as many people as possible so you arranged for it to be built on a major route, often just on the outside of the city or town walls. But here at a crossroads your tomb could be seen by people travelling on either route. And that's just what we had here – three Roman burial mounds by what seems to be a crossroads.

'Also ploughed out near here is a Bronze Age barrow is known to archaeologists as "G.6.b". The finds from it tell a really interesting story.'

'You'd never guess if they go around giving names like "G.6.b." Geez, they do make try to make prehistory sound like spare parts for a washing machine.'

'Be that as it may, what they found was a main burial in the middle… '

'As you might expect… '

'Indeed. But around were other burials, presumably added a little later. And most of these were infants. There's a drawing showing what they might have looked like in the Stables Gallery of the Alexander Keiller Musuem back in Avebury. Almost certainly there were a family group. I find it rather moving to look at that drawing – which is with some of the finds from the graves – and all-but look at a family who were living around here the best part of four thousand years ago.'

'It's only one step away from looking at a nineteenth century photograph of some "local farmer and his family".'

'Yes. For a start we seem to be seeing the same sorts of rates of infant mortality that we know would be typical until about a hundred years ago. On the other hand a nineteenth century Wiltshire farmer was probably more of a "local yokel" than the Bronze Age people as they were much more European in their outlook.'

'How do you mean?'

'Well, unlike the late Neolithic when there is little or no evidence for contact with Continental Europe – only with the west and north of the British Isles – by the early Bronze Age the designs of pottery are shared throughout western Europe and the British Isles. Only later in the Bronze Age does pottery become more "regional" again. So the implication is that for much of the Bronze Age we were much more in touch with the culture of mainland Europe than at any other time before the Romans.'

'And much more so than in the nineteenth century! We'd been at war with France and weren't that fond of the Prussians, Austrians, and all the other nations that were coming together as Germany.'

'Well, there's probably a good deal more that could be said about nineteenth century Anglo-European politics but, from the perspective of a Wiltshire farmer of the time, you've probably touched on the key issues! Hardly pioneers of a pro-EU outlook!'

'Anyway, didn't you say there were even more recent burials up here – Roman and Anglo-Saxon?'

'Yes. As often seems to have happened – although archaeologists weren't really looking out for the evidence until the 1980s – the Anglo-Saxons often placed burials into the sides of Bronze Age barrows, or in the ground close by. They even placed one in the most northerly of the Roman mounds.'

'So they knew that Bronze Age people were buried there? That doesn't seem right!'

'No, it's not. They presumably thought they were people who had been buried within a hundred or two years before, not more than two thousand years before. But back in the parts of northern Europe where the Angles and the Saxons and such like emigrated from, they had re-introduced the custom of burying under mounds. There may have been some borrowing of ideas from the Romans, but it's not really clear why.

'Whatever the full story, it would mean that when the Anglo-Saxons first settled in parts of England where there were Bronze Age barrows then they would – wrongly, but quite understandably – think that people like them had lived and died thereabouts.'

'So by burying their dead in what seemed to them to be "ancestral mounds" they would just continue their claim a right to live there? I wonder what the locals who were living there at the time made of that?'

The Sanctuary as it is now.

    'Sadly we don't know, but presumably "Not a lot!"'

'But yes,– even if we now know it is totally wrong – I can see how the Anglo-Saxons would have thought that "People like us buried their dead here, so we belong here too."'

'All this Bronze Age, Roman, Anglo-Saxon activity up here. But not a lot from the Neolithic?'

    'Wrong! Very wrong! But not burials. And we need to cross the modern road to see what's left. Take care and above all don't cross if you can hear something coming – the traffic's often doing over sixty miles an hour – and at that speed the stopping distance is way past how far you can see when driving up to the crest of the hill.'

Grid reference 118680

'Oh, this is a bit different. Concentric little henges made of concrete posts, with their tops painted different colours. The archaeologists have gone to town here – presumably there's really good story to tell!'

    'Yes all the posts do look like henges. And indeed there was a circle of fairly small stones here until the seventeenth century. The pioneering antiquarian William Stukeley made

87

The Sanctuary as drawn by William Stukeley in the early 1720s, shortly before the removal of the stone circle.

a sketch showing forty-two stones, but all the stones were taken away soon after in 1724. The archaeological dig showed there had once been two rings of stones, although one might have been before the other one. Most of these concrete posts show where there had been four concentric rings of big timber posts. It was Stukeley who gave it the name of The Sanctuary. This name has stuck although we shouldn't allow it to influence our ideas about its purpose in the Neolithic.'

'But we can see it was a really complicated building, with all these posts holding up a really big roof... '

'Perhaps. But perhaps we're looking at a series of circular structures built in succession as the previous one rotted or was ritually removed. And quite likely they were just circles of posts, and there never was a roof.'

'Didn't the archaeologists find enough evidence to work it all out?'

'Sadly not. The first excavation was in 1930 and, to put it politely, wasn't done all that well and the records are even worse. Another dig was organised in the 1999 found that the earlier excavation had missed quite a bit... '

'That suggests it wasn't that good... '

'Indeed. But although the later dig allowed for some radiocarbon dating and the like, it wasn't able to shed any real light on the detail. So there's been a lot of speculation about what went on here. If it was a big building then it could be where the "priests" lived or trained. One popular author implied it was where the rites of passage for young girls at puberty took place.'

'Which does seem to be telling us more about the author than the Neolithic!'

'Maybe. I was talking earlier about excarnation before burial and an elevated platform held up by sturdy posts such as these would be typical of excarnation platforms known from traditional societies which still used such funerary practices in recent times. But then we should be expecting to be finding human finger bones and toes bones – the sorts of bones that are small enough to get easily detached before the later burial phase.'

'But could it be that such small bones simply didn't survive as they'd be on or near the surface?'

'That is a real possibility. But a Dr Toope collected what he referred to as "bushels" of human bones from this area in the middle of the seventeenth century.'

'Was he studying them as archaeologists do now?'

'No, he was grinding them up to make what was thought at the time to be potent medicine. King Charles the Second was very fond of potions made from human skulls and such like.'

'Uhhh!'

'All around here has been disturbed by chalk digging and the transport café that used to be where the parking area is now. Much of the archaeology must have been lost.'

'So not much chance of coming up with a convincing idea as to what the Sanctuary really was.'

'Sadly not. But it is still a fascinating place, right at the prow of the "over" of Overton Hill.'

'Ah yes, I remember you were saying that "over" is the Anglo-Saxon's word for a hill that looks like an upturned canoe.'

'The River Kennet's right down there. You can see West Kennett chambered long barrow over there. East Kennett chambered barrow is that way. Silbury Hill and Swallowhead Springs are just behind Waden Hill – and it's that part down there where the smaller version of Silbury has been discovered. It's been nicknamed Silbaby although the archaeologists prefer to call it Waden Mound. We'll go there in a few minutes.

'Let's go back to the gate by the road. Before we move on just take a quick look at this Bronze Age barrow on this side of the road. It seems to belong with the ones we looked at earlier on the north side of the road. And presumably there were more where the road is now.

'We'll pick up this byway which drops down steeply. We're right at the "bows of the canoe" of the over. To our right older maps show the site of a small stone circle but archaeological surveys have failed to come up with any convincing evidence, so it might have been a more-or-less natural circle of sarsens.'

'A bit like Falkner's Circle which we looked at earlier on this walk?'

'Perhaps. But frankly whatever this might have been is now lost to us. It might have been important at some time but then again it might not.

'OK, when we get to the bottom we need to take the footpath to the right. But it's worth just taking a short detour down to the little wood and the attractive bridge over the River Kennet. It's a lovely little spot.'

Take the footpath running to the west (it starts at grid reference 119677) until you get to the road (grid reference 116677). Turn left then go over the bridge. Take care as this lane can be busy with traffic. Then take the footpath on the right, just after the little pumping station. Follow the path into the woodland then, just after signs on the left for the White Horse Way look out on the right for a rather hidden gap in the trees (grid reference 114678). Take this much narrower path heading north through the little wood until you get to a stile (grid reference 114679). Follow the path with the edge of the field on your left.

'Oh, look Bob, isn't that the River Kennet again just over to our right?'

'Yes. By the time we've got across this field we'll be even closer. But look the other way – what can you see?'

'That must be West Kennett long barrow – and it seems to be sitting exactly on the top of the hill!'

'I agree, and I don't think it's just coincidence that it's only down here by the river is where the barrow sits on the skyline so perfectly. If – as all the archaeological evidence suggests – Mesolithic and the early Neolithic people who built such long barrows made extensive use of boats, then anyone coming here is most likely to have come up the river, not by an overland route.'

'But wasn't everywhere covered in woodland back then? So you wouldn't see the barrow from down here?'

'It was just an assumption by archaeologists that everywhere was wooded. But clearing areas of trees by setting fire to them encourages the sort of plants to grow which attract deer and other wild herbivores, and are also very helpful if you've got cattle, sheep, goats, and such like. It seems likely that, even if most places were wooded, there were also clear areas too.'

'And, I suppose you're going to say that this view here from the river up to West Kennett long barrow right on the skyline is good evidence for just such a clearing?'

Indeed! I can see you're get the hang of this archaeological deduction malarky.

'How about I show you this sketch map *[see next page]* and see what you can deduce from that… '

'Oh, lots of curvy lines. But I can't see anything – it's just ploughed fields, and a few hedges, all the way past those modern farm buildings.'

'You're right, there's nothing to be seen. This is a plot based on crop mark photographs, geofiz surveys and just a little bit of excavation between 1987 and 1992. They mark out rows and ovals of holes for fairly massive timber posts which made so-called "palisaded enclosures". And each post seems to been put upright with its own ritual deposits of pig bones at the base. Presumably when they were placed there then there was meat on them, not just bare bones.'

'Hang on! I'm struggling to get my head around how big these are. They seem to be a bit bigger than the Sanctuary where we were a few minutes ago.'

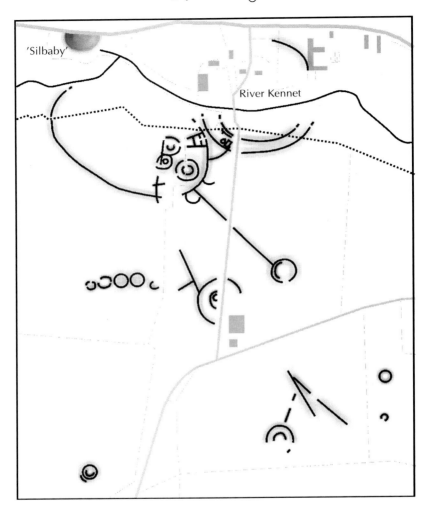

'Silbaby'

River Kennet

'Right – the biggest of the timber rings at the Santuary was twenty-one to twenty-two yards across. Here there were enclosures well over three hundred yards across. That's getting on for the size of the main henge at Avebury, which is about four hundred and fifty yards across. The guesstimate is that there were over four thousand fairly massive timber posts – which would have required clearing nearly a hundred acres of suitable woodland.'

'So no roofs here, that's for sure! But what were they for?'

'Silbaby' or Waden Mound.

Grid reference of farm buildings near the southern extent of the palisades 110677

'Well, whatever you can deduce is likely to be as good as any ideas anyone else has put forward. The presence of so much pig bone shouts out "Ritual!" – at least for the construction if not for the main use. There are funnel-like structures all the way over to those modern farm buildings and they look like they could have funnelled animals into the main enclosures. So just perhaps they were rounding up more-or-less wild pigs for a ritualised hunt inside the palisaded enclosures.

'Curiously the river seems always to have always run through the enclosures, which could have ritual or mythic significance. It would also be handing if people were living here, although I doubt they were here all year round.'

'You know, even though there's so little to see here, this place is beginning to really intrigue me! What with the visibility to both West Kennett chambered long barrow and the Sanctuary and – although you've not mentioned it yet – Silbury Hill first becoming visible from here, it's like everything that isn't directly linked with the henge or Windmill Hill seems to "happen" around here.'

'Indeed. I've not mentioned Silbury Hill yet partly because what we can see is later than anything else from the Neolithic – although there may have been something going on there *before* the hill was built. But what you can just make out from over here is Silbury's little "baby". It was only spotted in recent years and so far there's not been much archaeological investigation. But initial results suggest it's not natural and seems to have been built in the Neolithic. Most people I know call it Silbaby but the archaeologists have given it the grown up name of Waden Mound as it is on the very foot of Waden Hill.'

'We can walk up to it but need to go as far as that stile and use the bridge to get over.'

Walk to the path from West Kennett long barrow to the lay by and turn right to follow across the bridge (grid reference 104682). Then walk across the meadow towards Silbaby (grid reference 106683).

'Sometimes there is a spring flowing from the side of Silbaby, but it's all dry today.'

'What do we know about it?'

'Frankly, not a lot. It is in a direct line between Silbury Hill and the Sanctuary, which might be significant. There has been a very limited attempt to get dating evidence – which suggests it is Neolithic but doesn't get any clearer than that. Bear in mind it was only recognised as being of interest as recently as 2004, and as it wasn't a professional archaeologist who spotted it, it then took several years before any work was done.'

'Even though there was a whole team of professional archaeologists working on the palisaded enclosures right by it between 1987 and 1992? They must have been going around with their eyes closed as it is spot-on the same shape as Silbury Hill, just a lot smaller.'

'Presumably it was more overgrown then.'

'So, another intriguing part of this immediate area but just more questions and few answers.'

'Seems so.'

'Where next? Can I suggest West Kennett long barrow?'

West Kennett long barrow sits on the skyline when seen from the banks of the River Kennet.

Grid reference of bridge on path to West Kennett chambered long barrow 104682

'Yes – though just for once be prepared to see lots of other people around. It's a fairly easy stroll from the lay by and, no matter what time of day, there's almost always a steady stream of visitors. All we need to do is return to the little bridge and then follow the path through the kissing gate and uphill across the large open field. And don't be surprised when the long barrow dips below the horizon!'

Grid reference of West Kennett chambered long barrow 105678

'Now, have I got this right – the people who were building this chambered barrow were the same folk right at the start of the Neolithic who built the causewayed enclosure on the top of Windmill Hill.'

'Yes, that seems right. And just as Windmill Will continued being used through most or maybe all the Neolithic, so too ritual "depositions" were being made inside the barrow many hundreds of years after it came into existence.

'First of all the four side chambers were more-or-less blocked off. And after that these massive stones which form the façade were added. The dating evidence is at best

The façade of West Kennett long barrow soon after sunrise.

ambiguous but this was perhaps about four hundred years after the main phase of construction. Before that there was a more open forecourt and the entrance passage was clearly visible. The stones that were added visually block the entrance – although we know that a great many ritual "depositions" continue to be made, so access was still possible.'

'What sort of things went into these "depositions"?'

'Predictably enough there were large quantities of broken pottery. Because this is dateable we know that the top levels were nearly a thousand later than the oldest ones.'

'But that's longer than some of our cathedrals have been in use – Salisbury cathedral wasn't even built a thousand years ago, and even the really old ones like Winchester would have looked very different then to how they are now.'

'Yes, it is a long time. But there must have been some real continuity here as the pottery is always found with worked flint, bone tools and animal bone.'

'And all this was found inside the chambers?'

'Not forgetting human bones too. Although they were mostly in the older layers towards the bottom.'

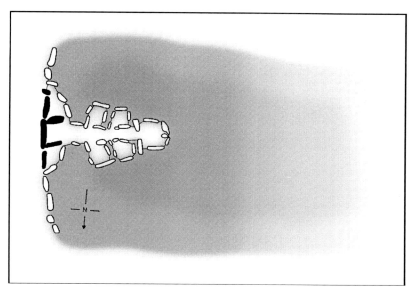

A plan of the eastern end of the West Kennett long barrow. The main chamber was created in the earlyNeolithic; the façade stones shown in solid black were added towards the end of the Neolithic. Archaeologists refer to them as the 'blocking stones'.

'You said earlier they were not burials. So they were just bones jumbled in with the broken pots and what have you.'

    'Well. Not always "jumbled up" – there was some order to whose bones were where. It'll be easier to explain when we go inside. But first I want you to get as feel for this place. It's more than just a chamber. Let's walk along the top to the far end. But first take a look to the remains of this ditch running along the length. There's another one on the other side. This is were the soil and chalk rubble came from to build the mound. Sadly it's been a bit encroached on by the ploughing but it's about as easy to make out as any of these surviving side ditches.

    'Ignore this depression just beyond the chamber – that seems to be just where a farmer dug some of it away.'

'Which direction are we walking in, Bob? I was wondering if the axis of the mound aligned with anything important like sunrises?'

'Well we're walking almost due west, which of course means the façade is almost due east, so the axis certainly seems to be intentionally aligned. But the sun rises due east only at the equinoxes. That might have been important in the Neolithic but there's no real evidence as the chamber tombs where there are really dramatic sunrise effects tend to be aligned with the midwinter sunrise. Here the midsummer sunrise only does something fairly subtle – it lights up one of the side chambers.

'Curiously, according to folklore collected in the nineteenth century, a white ghost appears here at dawn on midsummer, accompanied by a white hound with red ears. In the Welsh tales we know as the Mabinogion such hounds were linked with the goddess of the Otherworld, Annwn.'

'So, the entrance to this barrow thought to be an entrance to the Otherworld?'

'Just maybe. But until the excavations in 1859 I doubt if people really knew there was a way into the barrow – and not until 1956 could people just wander in, as we can now.

'But they were interested in the midwinter sunrise here too, as from this barrow that's when the sun rises over East Kennett long barrow.

'Of course the blocking stones now affect what happens. Before they were put up then around the equinoxes both the sun and the full moon would have shone all the way down the chamber just as they came up over the horizon.

'More interestingly, if that modern plantation of trees didn't block our view then we could see Morgan's Hill, the one where the transmission masts are. It's in line with the axis of the mound and, although it's not a big hill, there are two breast-like hillocks which might have had some symbolic significance.'

'Perhaps what is really significant is that the entrance faces in the same direction as the flow of the River Kennet and the Thames – so due east of here is the Thames estuary.'

'Seems at least as good as any suggestion!'

'It really is longer than I expected.'

'Well it is the longest of the known chamber tombs, though not as long as some unexcavated long barrows on Salisbury

Looking north-west to East Kennett long barrow (hidden by the tree clump in the middle distance). This photograph was taken from the Ridgeway to the south of East Kennett village. West Kennett long barrow is out of sight but almost in line with Silbury Hill.

Plain – though those probably never had chambers. Now we've reached the western end, just take a look over there.'

'Silbury Hill.'

'And what's beyond Silbury Hill?'

'Well it must be Windmill Hill. In fact the Bronze Age barrows on the top seem to be sitting on the shelf near the top of Silbury Hill! Of course – you pointed this out to me when we were on Windmill Hill.'

'Yes, But the odd thing is that Windmill Hill only sits on the "shelf" from this end of the barrow, not when looking from the façade end.'

'What's the significance of that?'

'No idea! Silbury Hill wasn't built until nearly 1,500 years after these long barrows and the causewayed camp. And the

Silbury Hill seen from the summit of Windmill Hill. The arrows point to the east and west ends of West Kennett long barrow. Similarly the Bronze Age barrows on Windmill Hill appear to sit on the 'shelf' near the summit of Silbury Hill if you stand at the western end (i.e. the end away from the chambers).

shelf is just as likely to be Ango-Saxon as Neolithic. But this long barrow appears to be on the side of Silbury when seen from the site of the all-but-lost Horslip long barrow, so perhaps the builders of Silbury still thought the barrows had significance.

'But the location of this long barrow seems to have important to the builders of the henge.'

'Why do you say that?'

'Well if I stretch one arm out towards the direction of the Avebury henge and then stretch my other arm out straight the other way... '

'Roughly to the south... '

'... then I'm pointing at Stonehenge.'

'An exact alignment of the three sites?'

'Yes, exact.'

'Interesting – almost a little too interesting!'

'Let's walk back to the façade and make our way inside.

'Before we get carried away with more speculative thoughts, remember the polisher stone we found in the henge? Here between the side chambers on the south side is an even more interesting example.'

'But you said that these were used for polishing before they would stood up. Yet this is inside an early Neolithic chamber tomb… '

'Exactly! I told you it was an interesting example – and that's why. It has to be have been used for polishing before the tomb was built around 3,650 BC. This is the only polisher stone so far discovered which can be dated so accurately.'

'It's a good example too – there are several quite big areas which have been rubbed smooth. Are there any other interesting stones?'

'Well one way of thinking about this place is that they're all interesting. We can see how the big stones were used to make a corbelled roof – even if the top part was replaced in the 1950s by a concrete skylight. And these sections of drystone walling fill in the gaps.'

So what do we know about the people who were buried here?'

'Hang on – remember what I said about the bones not being buried?'

'Ah yes – they were simply laid out on the ground in here… '

'Sadly we know too little about the remains. In 1685 Dr Toope of Marlborough dug into the mound and, as he proudly wrote to John Aubrey, "… stored myself with many bushels, of which I made a noble medicine that relieved many of my distressed neighbours." Then when the pioneering archaeologist John Thurnham excavated the main passage and the western chamber in 1859 he did not record the finds to anything like modern standards. But thankfully Thurnam simply missed the four side chambers, so when Stuart Piggott arrived here in 1955 to start a modern dig he was able to excavate those more thoroughly.

'First you need to get your head around the immense length of time that people were putting bodies and things in here. There's what are called the "primary deposits" and they include the remains of about thirty people. This seems to cover just a few generations. But after that – for nearly a thousand years – human and animal bones, flint tools, pieces of pots and presumably a whole host of now-lost organic remains were being added.'

'What do we know about the human remains from the primary deposits?'

'There seems to have been just one complete skeleton. There were what appeared to be other more-or-less complete skeletons but, when the bones were looked at more closely, they turned out to be a mix from several different persons. The best estimate is that the bones of at least thirty people were placed here. The most recent radiocarbon dating suggests the majority are from the same generation or two from around the time when the barrow was constructed – around 3,650 BC. But a few are several hundred years later. And some remains, mostly children, were added from 3,300 BC to possibly as recently as 2,500 BC.'

'Why so few people?'

'We can only assume there was something special about the people whose bones came to be in here. But whether they were revered or feared is an open queestion. Quite clearly there were some after-death rituals as there were clear differences between whose bones were in which side chambers.'

'Such as?'

'When Thurnham dug this main chamber to the west he found an infant's skull and five male burials. One was a teenager, two were in their early thirties and another who was about fifty when he died. There was also one arm, the lower jaw and a few other bones of a middle-aged man. With them were pottery, stone tools, a bone pin and a stone bead.

'Piggot found bones in all four side chambers. He also found cremated remains in north-west corner of the north-east chamber. The bones were rather mixed together. Interestingly, fewer skulls than would be expected from the number of other bones were found. And not enough long bong bones from legs and arms.

The polisher stone inside West Kennett long barrow. When used to polish stone axes it would have been horizontal, so the polished areas must have been created before it was incorporated into the monument.

'Some of the remains were less disturbed than others. In the south-east chamber over there the people tended to be younger and more equally of both sexes. One adult man and woman were found lying together with a fragment from a pottery bowl between them. Nearby was a jumble of many infant bones including a foetus of five or six months gestation. Artefacts included pins, needles and scoops made from bone.

'What about this chamber to the south-west?'

'Piggot was able to identify nine adults, a youth, a child and two infants. Also animal bones from oxen, sheep or goats, pigs, dogs, a jackdaw and a polecat.

'Opposite, to the north-west was mostly lots of disarticulated bones. Just one young adult male was still articulated. And here in the north-east was the clearest example of a later burial as an old man had been placed on his left side on stone slabs partially above a burial that was between five hundred and a thousand years earlier. The old man might have been killed by the flint arrow head found near his throat.'

'So the chambers were full of human remains?'

'No, the bones were mostly at or near bottom. Above them was masses of deliberately placed chalk rubble, with broken pottery, flint tools, pieces of sarsen and what archaeologists describe as "humic soil".'

'That suggests there was lots of plants and such like too.'

'Indeed the depositions almost certainly included food plants and flowers, although there is of course no direct evidence.'

'These would presumably have been brought from where they were living… '

'What really interests me is that these secondary deposits seem to have continued for about a thousand years – long after the so-called "blocking stones" were placed across the forecourt.'

'So people were coming in here, moving the bones about – no doubt as part of a ritual that was meaningful and profound for them – and leaving all sorts of plants, food, broken pots, and what have you. It must have been quite eerie, as there would have been little light, probably just some sort of flickering torches.'

'Indeed. And by flickering torch light the stones come alive.'

'Not literally I hope!'

'Perhaps not literally, but certainly in a way that would have been convincing. At least eight of the stones look like human faces or skulls.'

'But isn't that just one step removed from seeing things in flickering flames?'

'I'd be inclined to agree except that all the faces are looking south and two of them are in really prominent places – right at the end of the main western chamber where they catch the light from the rising sun and moon at the equinoxes. I really don't think that's coincidence.

'Anyway – clap hands a few times!'

Simulacra at the western end of the chamber. The so-called 'living head' is to left with the 'skull stone' to the right. Both are seen better by flickering torch light than by the diffuse ambient light. Equinox sunrise lights up back wall with both head and skull stones. A shaft of sunlight shines on skull stone about fifteen minutes after sunrise at the equinoxes.

'Well, yes, interesting. But I suppose you would get good echoes in a place shaped like this.'

> 'Agreed. Now stand right in front of this skull simulacra and clap again. '

'Oh! It's different – kind of deeper and more resonant. Yes I'm beginning to agree that perhaps these simulacra aren't just "accidental"! So whatever rituals were doing on must have involved sound as well as the darkness and flickering lights.'

> 'Yes. And the size of chamber tombs is just right to resonate with the human voice chanting or singing. And don't forget that it would have a fairly powerful smell – even just the plants and food rotting long after the bones had become dry and almost odourless.
>
> 'And there is just a hint of evidence for making music here. Some of the ox bones that were found here – the phalanges

from the feet – seem to have been drilled in ways that would make them work like whistles or ocarinas.'

'Wow! You know, I can see this place being used for vision quests or shamanic initiations. It would have been really scary to have been places in here for, say, three days and three nights – or whatever – with only the bones of the ancestors for company, and a drum to communicate with the spirits.'

'Yes, well, there's a great many people who think that way. However, despite vast amounts of wishful thinking and bending of the evidence, there's no real evidence that people in northern Europe followed any sort of "shamanic" practices as we know them from Siberia, North America and the Sámi people. But even if though there's no evidence that stands up to scrutiny, in recent years it's become a deeply-seated belief that Neolithic people were "shamanic".

'But I must admit that the idea of undergoing a "ritual death" before being "reborn" is tempting. Clearly this monument is a tomb. But the layout of the five chambers is like a figure lying down – with the entrance between the legs.'

'You don't have to be called Sigmund to see the significance of that! So a "womb-tomb"? After all there are plenty of parallels in non-Western religion of powerful female deities who are both live-givers and death-dealers – so right now perhaps we're inside the body of a Neolithic goddess?'

'If you like. But, as ever with such speculations, there's no evidence!'

'This is just such an interesting place! But if you don't mind me saying so, I really think we need to get back out into the daylight. What else is there around here that you want to show me? Obviously Silbury Hill but is there anywhere else?'

Grid reference of bridge 104682

'Well, indeed there is Simon! But as we start to walk back down the hill to the kissing gate and the little bridge I want to share some speculations with you. Look over at that flat area to the left of the bridge between the trees over to the east and the main road.. Well, although it's difficult to make out now, the slight humpy-bumpyness in this field is the remains of a water meadow – or so-called "floating meadow" – which was a elaborate system of ditches and sluices which enabled the grass to be flooded at the end of the winter. This fertilised the soil and also created the right conditions for an early flush of grass for the sheep, at a time of year when the main fields would have not started growing again.'

'That would be when – a few hundred years ago?'

'Yes, best keep it vague as water meadows first start being created in the sixteenth century and remained in use until the early twentieth century. Most likely these ones are eighteenth century. But they needed regular maintenance and tweaking so the oldest parts may well have been re-dug and redone several times.

'But, bearing in mind that beavers weren't extinct in this country until the fourteenth century, I'd like to speculate about how this area might have been like before that. While beavers were around they must have been building dams and such like, so I'm tempted to think that it would only take a moderately industrious beaver colony to dam up the water somewhere near Silbaby and this whole flat area would be a lake.'

'So even when the river has stopped flowing in the summer and autumn there would be still be water available… '

'And if you're bringing lots of cattle and other livestock up here, you must, must, must have reliable water during the summer – it's no good trying to rely on a stream that only runs in the winter! If my thoughts about beavers are even partway right they would be doing the Neolithic farmers a big favour!'

'So there would be a lake in the midst of all these ritual monuments – a sacred lake then, perhaps?'

'Now, funny you should say that, because there was certainly a sacred spring. Indeed there still is. Now we're through the kissing gate just head for the little bridge but then turn sharp left and walk along the edge of the field with the river on your left.'

Grid reference of bridge 104682

'Now look at those trees on the far bank… '

'They're on a little cliff.'

The stepping stones near Swallowhead spring. The Winterbourne is flowing in from the left and becomes the River Kennet as it turns the corner. London and the Thames estuary are a (long way) out of sight beyond the horizon!

'Yes that's because the rock changes. This part of the chalk is slightly harder and so the river has cut up to it but not eroded it very much. Can you see over there, more or less in front of us, there's another little cliff with not quite as many trees? They meet just out of sight to our left.

'Keep walking and head round the corner to where there's a stile.'

Grid reference 101681

'Ah. There's big stepping stones across to the other side.'

'Yes. I've no idea when they were put there but it's since the 1980s. Stand in the middle and look in the direction we've walked from.

'This is the start of the River Kennet – follow the water downstream and you'll meet up with the Thames at Reading then flow on into the North Sea. Give or take a few bends it's due east all the way.

'The water flowing down to the stepping stones from the north is the Winterbourne. And can you see the little stream bed running under that bent-over willow branch... '

'The one with all the ribbons and other stuff tied to it... '

'That's the one. That's the run off from Swallowhead Springs. Just take the rise to the left and climb up the cliff then follow to the right. We can then drop back down to where the spring itself is.'

'Oh this is a really magical sort of place. I can see why the pagans have adopted that tree.'

'OK, as there's no water at this time, just walk down the streambed to where that willow branch bends over... '

'Oh I'm having another Freudian moment – it's as if I'm squeezing out from you-know-where and being born again... '

'Perhaps we should have done a bit of a ritual ourselves then!'

'Down here where the little cliffs meet, and the trees are above us, it's so secluded. I think this is one of the most interesting places you've brought me to so far. What was going on here in the Neolithic?'

'We've no idea. Frankly no one took much interest in this place until Michael Dames featured it his books *Silbury Treasure* and *Avebury Cycle* which were published in the late 1970s. Soon after modern pagans – mostly women's groups, such as those associated with the Greenham Common protest camp – started to come here. But there's never been any archaeological investigation.'

'I'll talk a bit more about the possible significance of this spring to Neolithic people when we get over to Silbury Hill. But it is only speculation!'

'Let's go back over the stepping stones and the stile.

'Although I said this field here might have been part of a lake, what we do know is that there were Roman buildings and what were either deep wells here – though they seem to have been used more for making ritual deposits than as sources of water. Indeed in the field to the west – just beyond the Winterbourne and the little cliff with trees – there's evidence of a small Roman town. The best guess is

The willow tree where Simon has a 'Freudian moment'.

that there was a temple – presumably in some way linked to Silbury Hill.'

'And the modern A4 follows the line of the Roman road from London to Bath.'

'Yes, right here the modern road is close to the Roman road, although they deviate within a few hundred yards to both east and west. If you take a look at the OS map you will see dotted lines marking the line of the Roman Road.

'Rather handily this town is ten miles in each direction from two other Roman towns. To the west was Verlucio, which was at Sandy Lane near Calne. The other to the east was called by the Romans Cunetio and was right by a place written as Mildenhall but pronounced "My-null".'

'Ten miles is a common distance between Roman towns – presumably it was as far as the soldiers were expected to walk in a day?'

'Maybe. It was as far as an ox cart could do in a day, although only half what a lightly-equipped messenger might walk in a day, and the third of a distance where a messenger riding a horse in a hurry would need to change mounts.'

'Ah, but all rather handy whichever means of transport you're using. What have they dug up here?'

'Not a lot! It was discovered by geofiz as recently as 2000 or 2001 and only a few trial trenches and such like have been dug. They confirmed that the geofiz anomalies are Roman, but beyond that we're left guessing.'

'But presumably it was there because of Silbury Hill, just over there?'

'Well that's a good guess. One of the geofiz results suggests a temple. And then there's the ritual deposits from the deep wells or shafts excavated a long time ago. But that's about as far as the facts go.'

'This is one of the places where Silbury Hill looks quite impressive. It's odd that such a big mound was built in a the one part of the landscape where it is least visible from the other prehistoric sites!'

'Isn't it just!'

'Presumably this is one of the most excavated of the Neolithic sites around here.'

'Yes indeed. Partly because there have been three different attempts to dig into the middle of it, not that they found much. But more especially because those earlier tunnels and shafts were very poorly back-filled so in 2000 a hole appeared in the top of Silbury Hill. The outcome was a combination of archaeological investigation and massive repairs.'

'When were the earlier digs? I assume that antiquarians thought that this was a very big burial mound and therefore someone important – with lots of grave goods – would be underneath.'

'That seems to be pretty much what they thought. There was even a bit of folklore that said that King Sil – sometimes spelt as Zil – had been buried under there on a golden horse.'

'Ah – so Silbury Hill takes its name from an otherwise unknown king called Sil.'

'As if! It seems likely that the Anglo-Saxons put a fort on top – which would explain why it's flat at the top now and is certainly where the "bury" part of the name comes from as that is from the Old English "burh" meaning, among other things, a defensive earthwork. So, although it appears in

Beyond the Henge

early records as Seleburh, which would mean something like the "hall fort", there's a good chance it was known more informally as "King's Hill" or maybe the "King's Hill burh".'

'And anyone saying "King's Hill" in a Wiltshire dialect would sound like they're saying "King Sil". Yes I can see how that legend might arise!'

'Anyway, to answer your question. There was a shaft dug down from the top in 1776. A tunnel was dug in 1849 and some other excavations took place in 1886. And then the tunnel was re-dug in 1968 for a well-publicised TV series.'

'What did they find?'

'Next to nothing. The only recorded find from 1776 was a thin slip of oak wood from the bottom of the shaft. It could well have been associated with a void left by a very large timber post. The 1849 tunnel established that the mound was constructed from turf and chalk rubble – they still have one of those bits of turf in Devizes Museum. The report of the time notes that in the top of the turf there was moss – which still looked fresh and retained its colour – and snail shells. There were also some pieces of sarsen, animal bone and antler tines.

'Digs in 1867 and 1896 were simply to find out whether Silbury Hill is on top of the Roman road or whether the road diverted around it. A number of eminent people were adamant that it was later than the Roman period and so were no doubt a little miffed when the evidence clearly showed that the Roman road surface went around Silbury Hill.

'We now know that Silbury Hill is about four and half thousand years old.'

'That means it was standing longer *before* the Romans than the time between the Romans and us! Presumably the 1969 TV series was when lots of finds were discovered?'

'Well clearly the sheer cost of bringing all the live outside broadcasting equipment to here – remember that there was little in the way of recording equipment then other than film – let alone the funding the excavations themselves was all based on decisions about how much "treasure" might be found. But once again very little was discovered except more details about the construction.

112

Silbury Hill at sunset.

'The TV series even started one bit of duff information that is still frequently repeated as fact.'

'What's that?'

'Well when they looked closely at the old turf they found not only moss and snail shells but also dead insects. Among them were winged ants – but a species that only flies in early August. So it was suggested that the turves had been cut in August.'

'Seems reasonable!'

'No it's not! Soon after growing wings the ants die. Their bodies do not decompose quickly so *whenever* you dug up the turf there would be dead winged ants in there.'

'Ah, see the point. So Silbury Hill wasn't built in a month, least of all in August.'

'Well, it might have been built in August just as easily as any other month – but the dead ants shouldn't be considered as evidence. But any number of web sites still tell you it was built in August!'

'And it was this tunnel which collapsed in 2000?'

'Well the BBC's tunnel mostly followed the 1849 tunnel, which had never been back-filled at all. And no attempt was made to properly refill the 1776 shaft – there are photos of the BBC team looking up into that void. So for a combination of reasons the hill was not really stable.'

'What happened when the hole in the top was discovered?'

'Well fairly quickly some quick fixes were made. But it took several years of surveys followed by collective head-scratching at English Heritage to decide the right course of action. Not until 2007 did anything really obvious kick in.'

'Was the aim just to stabilise the hill or did they try to do some more archaeology?'

'Oh they had a good crack at the archaeology as well! This time they managed to get a peek at what was there before the hill was built.'

'And?'

'Well, a central mound of gravel and turves about a yard high and ten yards across. And there were several smaller mounds nearby but how many is not known as the repair work didn't cut into where they all might have been. And into these mounds small pits had been dug and then filled in almost immediately. This first phase was radiocarbon dated quite accurately to 2400 BC, give or take about 50 years. Then the central mound was expanded into something slightly bigger – about five or six yards high and over thirty-five yard across.

'So the one big monument we see now is the successor to a series of much smaller mounds. I didn't know that.'

'Well no one did until the 2007 dig. And even then it wasn't well known until the book about the dig came out in 2010. The mound was surrounded by a massive ditch seven yards deep and almost as wide.'

'A bit like a small henge, then.'

'Similar except there was at least one big gap in the ditch. What's really odd is that not long after this massive ditch had been dug it was filled in as another such ditch was dug slightly further out. And then they did the same thing again. Only when they did this a fourth time do we get the ditch which is still visible – although much silted up.'

'And that's when the mound as we see it now was built?'

'Yes. And there are some cleverly placed walls of stone rubble radiating from the centre which kept the whole structure stable while it was being built, and have contributed greatly to ensuring it is still standing 4,500 years later. If you want to find out all the ins and outs then you'll need to read the excellent book that the two leading archaeologists wrote. It's called *The Story of Silbury Hill*.'

'How much has it changed over the millennia?'

'The main shape seems more or less as it always was, although most likely the top was more rounded rather than flat. Of course there's no evidence of what was there but it does seem it was flattened by the Anglo-Saxons who built a small fort up there.'

'So the "Keep Out" signs are to make sure that people's feet don't wear it away.'

'That's important too. But it's also important for the plants and insects that live on the slopes and they are even more easily damaged.

'If we make our way along the footpath at the side of the A4 and then either pop through this little wood or follow the path around it then we'll get to a good viewing place.'

Grid reference of viewing area 097686

'You get a good view not only of the mound but the ditch too.'

'Yes the ditch must have been much more than just a source of soil and chalk to make the mound. It must have been thought of as part of part of the 'grand plan'.

'Does it flood?'

'Surprisingly – considering it's dug into chalk – it still does. The Beckhampton stream flows into it from our left. The course of that stream also drains into the Winterbourne, although these days it has to be a very wet winter before it starts to flow.'

'Wasn't it you wrote about Silbury Hill being like a primordial creation mound?'

'Well I took most of a whole book to being to outline the reasons why! But I took my cue from the English Heritage archaeologists who, in their book *The Story of Silbury Hill*, simply said that while the Neolithic people were building it they must have been telling – and retelling – a very important myth.

'Because creation myths involving primordial mounds are found throughout the world it seemed likely that a version of this myth would be the most likely one here in the Neolithic. I wove in a whole load of other comparisons with worldwide folklore and myth to give this suggestion a bit more substance.

'One of the associated ideas is about the idea of a world tree or *axis mundi*. These are at least as commonplace as primordial mounds and often go together. Above all, such world trees are often by the side of a sacred spring or lake. One of the Scandinavian sagas talks of the world tree – known to the Norse as Yggdrasill – having its roots watered with white silt. The other descriptions say that it had a well at its roots. And that well is sometimes linked with swans.

'Ah, so that would fit very well with Silbury on the chalk and with Swallowhead Springs – and also with your suggestions that there might have been a lake there too.'

'And with the eighteenth century discovery of what might have once been a large timber post at the centre of the base of Silbury Hill.'

'And maybe the post hole at the south entrance to the henge or even Seahenge from the north Norfolk coast?'

'Well, don't get too carried away! But yes, world trees and their like do appear rather often down the ages.'

'And that's all in your book *Singing Up the Country*?'

'Yes, along with much more. For example, if you stand right here in August then the full moon appears to rise up from the small causeway on the south side by the road.

'No doubt we could stay here all day speculating about what it all meant. As you said before, the Neolithic people themselves probably had more than one way of thinking about it all, and those ideas would keep on evolving and adapting.'

'Indeed. Make your way back to the car park and from there we need to take this footpath which runs around the north-west side of the ditch. As you can see it will take us towards the side of Waden Hill – the opposite side to where the West Kennett Avenue runs.

Silbury Hill with the August full moon rising.

'Interestingly, quite a bit of evidence of Roman buildings and even some burials were found when they dug a sewer pipeline across the lower slopes of Waden Hill in the 1990s. They seem to be associated with the Roman town subsequently discovered to the south of Silbury Hill in 2001. But any books written before 2001 then refer to this area as on Waden Hill as the Roman settlement.'

'So, if I'm right the Winterbourne is flowing along this side of Waden Hill. And you're saying the Roman stuff was found on the lower slopes of Waden Hill which are the other side of the Winterbourne from Silbury Hill?'

Grid reference of bridge over Winterbourne 101689

'Yes that's were the pipeline ran. When we get to that little bridge we can stop and imagine what it might have looked like in Roman times.

'Once we've crossed the bridge we need to go right at the path. If we just turned left and followed the path then we'd get back to the main visitors' car park near the henge. But I want to nip over the stile and walk up to the top of Waden Hill instead. It's a bit steep but not really difficult to climb.

Grid ref for stile: 107683

If you prefer instead to walk along the path beside the Winterbourne this will bring you back, along level ground, to the main visitors' car park at Avebury. This is also the start of fourth walk – see page 131.

'Ah – Waden Hill. That's a name to conjure with! The Anglo-Saxons thought it was the hill of Woden or Odin.'

> 'Oh no they didn't – although I know that's what it says in all sorts of books. The name is Anglo-Saxon alright – but the early spellings show it was from *weoh don.* It's the hill with the *weohs* on it.'

'Come on Bob, you know I'm not fluent in Old English! What's a *weoh*?'

> 'Well it's a word that means both "idol" and "shrine". Think of a statue of the Virgin Mary or another saint by the roadside in a Catholic country. It's a shrine because there's a statue there – and just placing the statue there creates a shrine. *Weoh* has that same double meaning – without the idol there is no shrine but by placing an idol you've created a shrine.'

'Right, so the Anglo-Saxons had statues which they placed by the side of their roads.'

> 'Just so. Except they may have been fairly crude – perhaps in both senses of the word – by the standards of later sculpture. Several places in England are now called Weeford and mean just that – the *weoh* by the ford.'

'So helping to protect a traveller who is crossing a ford that's running rather high, and such like.'

> 'Presumably. Here I think it's a little different and the *woehs* were on burial mounds.'

'Can't say I can see any from here.'

> 'No, they were all ploughed out before archaeologists got to them. But crop mark photographs and some geofiz have identified a fairly large cluster at the top of the hill here, and others further along the summit. Chances are they were

mostly or all Bronze Age but almost certainly the Anglo-Saxons would have reused them. And, in places where well-preserved Anglo-Saxons barrows have been excavated, there is sometimes evidence for a timber post in the centre.'

'And you're thinking that such posts would have been carved into idols?'

'Yes. No direct proof as such wooden carvings simply don't survive. But it would explain why a hill with a lot of *weohs* on top came to be called the *weoh don* or 'weoh hill'.

'Who would have been buried here? Just people from the immediate area?'

'Maybe. More likely it was the central sacred site for a whole tribe of people known as the Canningas. The villages of Bishops Cannings and All Cannings near Devizes derive from this, although the Canningas territory perhaps stretched as far north, west and east as those villages are to the south of here.'

'That would be to the other side of Marlborough and the other side of Calne.

'Yes.'

'Could Canningas be anyway related to Kennet?'

'Seems unlikely. But *Canningas* means "the people of Cana" so the Anglo-Saxon name Cana just might have evolved from a very much older name. But you could never prove it.'

'Cana was their original tribal leader then?'

'So all the text books say. Personally I think it could just as easily be the name of local deity – the guardian of the land if you like – that they all followed.

'As in Cann*ing*as – but you said that meant "people of".

'But you can be the people of a deity just as easily as the people of a human leader. And if the leader claimed descent from the deity – just as Anglo-Saxon kings of England claimed descent from Woden – there might be little difference! But I know the place-name experts would burn me for heresy for saying so!'

'So anyone buried here – with their grave marked by a *weoh* – would most likely one of the tribal leaders.'

The hawthorn tree on the side of Waden Hill adopted by pagans for offerings.

'Well, that's certainly likely. If so, we should be thinking of Waden Hill as a regionally important cult centre, not just the pagan equivalent to the village churchyard.'

Grid reference 106688

'Must admit, now that we're at the top, apart from a rather good view over the top of Silbury Hill there's not a lot to be seen.'

'Agreed! But that's because we're here in the middle of the day. Try walking up from Silbury Hill just after sunset at full moon.'

'And?'

'The moon just sits on the top of this hill and seems to big that you only need to walk a little further to reach out and touch it.'

'Sounds rather magical. But then you'd be up here, where all the burial mounds were, after dark. That sounds spooky.'

'Well it's just what someone who wanted to do a bit of divination or prophecy is likely to have done. The Anlgo-

Saxons had a phrase which literally means 'sitting out' but the implication was you sat at night on a burial mound or by a crossroads – and, as we saw at Seven Barrows on Overton Hill , best of all there may be burial mounds at a crossroads – and waited for visions.

'And if your way of thinking is that stars are the souls of the dead then sitting up here on a clear night with the sky "alive with souls" would be a very moving experience.'

'So you think people were "sitting out" in this way up here? Presumably that's before Christianity?'

'I've no idea if they were doing it here. But if we read between the lines of late Saxon law codes, people were still doing it fairly often as late as the eleventh century. After that the evidence really does peter out. But chances are that this would have been thought of as a good place to do such rituals.

'Anyway, let's drop down the slope here. There's some real evidence of paganism still going on here… '

'Ah, yes another tree with ribbons and such like, just like the one at Swallowhead.

'And the beech trees at the eastern entrance to the henge. Here's hoping all their spells come true!'

'Interesting view from here of the West Kennet Avenue, and the Bronze Age barrows up by the Ridgeway.'

Grid reference 108691

'Yes, it's a view I never tire of seeing. Head for the gates in the corner by the little lay by and we'll make our way back to the henge along the Avenue.'

'Does the Avenue really stop like that? I assume that's just where the archaeologists stopped.'

'You're partly right – the Avenue as we see it is because Alexander Keiller excavated the stones and re-erected them in the 1930s. But curiously geofiz suggests that there was originally some sort of break in the Avenue a few hundred yards south of where the stones now stop. But then they continue again – if you look at the road you can see it passes between two smallish stones.'

The Avenue looking north-west towards the henge. Taken at sunrise on summer solstice.

'And that's all that's left standing of the rest of the Avenue?'

'Yes.'

'Did Keiller find anything which dates the construction?'

'Not really – partly because he was working before modern dating techniques had been invented. But there's good reason to think that the Avenue – at least in it's final form – was put up after the henge but before Silbury Hill. That puts it around 2,600 or just a century or two after that. But frankly there's no hard evidence by which to date the Avenue.

'You know here we are walking down between the two rows as if it's a processional way. But when the Avenue was built this whole landscape was covered in sarsen stones. Maybe the way between the stones wasn't as clear then.'

'Or maybe it was clear – and if it was the only clear route it would have been the only way sarsens could have been dragged to the henge. If so perhaps it was as much a memory of the effort needed to build the henge as it was for living people to process along.'

'That's just possible. But perhaps it never was for people at all.'

'How to do you mean? Not even some sort of élite people, even if the more middling sort had to keep out?'

'Perhaps it was marked out so the souls of the dead could pass along unhindered. Just look at all the Bronze Age barrows on Overton Hill and think of the ones which have gone from Waden Hill. Although they date from many

The 'summer solstice sunrise stone' photographed soon after sunrise on the summer solstice.

centuries after the Avenue was constructed, remember what I was saying about Iron Age people seemingly thinking of Avebury as a taboo place. It's just as likely to be the same sort of place for the dead as has been suggested for Stonehenge.

'By the way, have you spotted that this stone seems to be pointing the wrong way?'

'Why's that?'

'Well, as Keiller seems to have been fairly reliable in putting them back the right way we have to assume it really was like that originally. And, if so, then someone deliberately put it up to point at the midsummer sunrise as it appears over the Ridgeway. It's one of the very few clear astronomical alignments anywhere in the Avebury monuments.'

'Interesting that the stones mostly alternate between tall fairly pointy ones and squarer ones. And that the two rows pair up pointy and

Falkner's Circle from the Avenue.

squarer ones. Is it just me or are they really intended to be male and female?'

    'No, it's not just you – plenty of other people, including Keiller himself, thought that. But whether the Neolithic people thought that is of course an open question. And, even if they did think in roughly those ways, it doesn't mean that they didn't think it symbolised something else as well.'

'Oh, you do make things complicated.'

    'Well, think how complicated our modern ideas about symbolic meanings can be. They're almost always at several "levels" and vary according to who is offering their opinion. Why should people less than five thousand years be any different?

    'Anyway, whatever they thought about them they chose to set them up almost exactly the same distance apart. The two rows are about fifteen yards apart and the stones in each row are between twenty and thirty yards apart.

Grid reference for Falkner's Circle 110694

    'Anyway, all this talking means we're missing some of what can be seen. Look just over there – can you make out the surviving stone from Falkner's Circle?'

'Ah yes, we saw it from the other side when we set off.'

'Now, over here are some more of Keiller's concrete markers.'

'Ah yes, where stones are missing.'

'Look out for one that's different.'

'Do you mean the one with a flat top instead of a point?'

'That's the one.'

'So it marks a flat-topped stone?'

'No! It marks where there wasn't a stone.'

'Keiller couldn't find any evidence at all for a stone? Had it been ploughed out or something?'

'No. There never was a stone. But what Keiller did find there was massive amounts of flint tools – over a thousand. There were even pits cut into the midden into which such items as a cattle skull and antlers had been ritually deposited.'

'Is midden a posh name used by archaeologists for a rubbish tip?'

'No. It's where people carefully placed things that "went out of use". We can't be sure they thought of them as "rubbish". They may have been more like offerings, or at least a way of linking their lives with ancestral claims to the place. We know the Scottish Travellers also deposited treasured items that no longer worked or were no longer needed in special places close their to favourite annual camp sites. If, some years later, they rummaged through and came across what to you and me might well seem like "rubbish" they could bring back memories of now-dead relatives who had once treasured the object.

'But really the main thing we learn from them is perhaps less about what is there than the insight it provides into the way lots of Neolithic people must have gathered together in the same places for many generations.'

'There's nothing to see now. But do we know how big it was?'

'This one was about a hundred yards long and forty yards wide. The deposits started being put there around 3,000 BC – which is well before they thought about building the Avenue. Rather than move it or anything they simply left it in place instead of putting a stone up.'

The midden is marked by the only square-topped concrete marker.

'Presumably if there's a big rubbish heap then they must have been least coming back each year to camp here.'

'Tempting thought. And I know it's tempted some archaeologists too. With any luck they'll shed some light on that soon.'

'Oh, that sounds exciting!'

'Well, that all depends what they find! Keiller was really only interested in excavating near the stones, but he did discover some human remains. It's not really clear what was going on but there do seem to be groups of partial human skeletons near the base of several of the stones, but outside the Avenue itself. But they are not the people who made the midden in the early Neolithic as the pottery with the burials tells that they lived right at the end of the Neolithic just before the Bronze Age.'

'So the stones became something like tombstones for a particular clan? I can just see some sort of geometrical designs such as you see

Approaching the henge. Except the henge is hidden by the rising ground...

on the pots painted on the flat side of the stones so folk know exactly which is where their ancestors are... '

    'Now you are getting far too speculative. Heraldry is not something we normally associate with the Neolithic... '

'You're just taking the mickey now...

    'Maybe, maybe not. Anyway, look ahead. How much of the henge can you see?'

'None! There's a little hill in the way.'

    'Interesting isn't it that one of the biggest henges we know of is invisible from about half a mile away.'

'You don't think it's just coincidence?'

    'No – the approaches to Stonehenge from the Cursus and avenues towards several smaller henges in northern Britain all show the same clever use of topography.'

'But when we get to the skyline we'll see the henge?'

    'Well, keep on walking and find out.'

Grid reference 104696

'Ah, yes suddenly we get to see the henge and the village. That really is quite an impressive way to approach it!'

A typical pair of 'male and female' stones.

OK, two things. Firstly, take a good look at these stones on the skyline and remember their shape.'

'Well, they're much like the other stones as far as I can tell. Actually a rather good pair of "male and female" ones.'

'That's all you need to remember. Now let's walk on between the markers.'

'Yes, lots of Keiller's concrete markers and not a lot of stones here. Presumably these were the first to go when people wanted stone to build their cottages and such like?'

'So it seems. But where is this stretch of the Avenue heading?'

'Well, it's turned left. Then it turns right again just near the end. It's like a snake wriggling.'

'Well, snake or not, is it taking us direct to the henge?'

'No – anything but!'

'If we just kept going and going in this direction where would we end up?'

The 'genii cuculatti' stones seen from the henge.

'Oh, I've no idea. Might be anywhere. Over there on the skyline is Windmill Hill... '

'Interesting, eh? This part of the Avenue seems to be "nodding" to the very earliest part of the monuments even though we know it is "really" heading to the henge.'

'And you don't think it's just coincidence?'

'Well who knows for sure. But there's every reason to think it was important to the people who put the stones up.

'Now, remember I asked you to remember the shape of the stones on the skyline back there? Look at them again now...'

'Hey, if I didn't know they were the same stones I really wouldn't recognise them. They're edge on and – well more like people.'

'Come here on a misty morning and it's just as if they're grey hooded figures. I like to think they're mourners for the souls passing along the Avenue into the henge.'

'Almost like people talk about seeing the ghosts of medieval monks in their grey habits with their cowls up.'

The last surviving pair of stones in the Avenue. Concrete markers show where now-missing stones once stood. This part of the Avenue seems to be leading towards Windmill Hill on the skyline as much as the henge in the middle distance.

'Or, if you go back to the Roman period, the sculptures of three *genii cucullati*, the local spirits – or *genii loci* – wearing the hooded robe known as a *culcullus*.

'Anyway, who knows what the Neolithic people made of them. Back to the present day – head to the gate in the corner and we'll cross the road over to the clump of beech trees at the southern entrance.

'Try to imagine that the entrance through the henge bank was originally a little further over to the right... '

'Where the beech trees are now?'

'Yes. And then aim towards the middle of those two really large stones.'

'So you're taking me as near as possible along the line of the original entrance?'

'Yes.'

This part of the walk retraces part of the Second Walk – see page 55 onwards.

130

Fourth walk

This walk is about half a mile but will take between half an hour and an hour depending on how much time is spent looking around the church.

Grid reference of cart park entrance 100696. See map on page 24.

'Right, Simon, come right over here towards the entrance to the main car park – just stand out of the way of the traffic. You're now looking at an Anglo-Saxon village.'

'I think you really mean "the site of an Anglo-Saxon village"!'

"Well, yes. Not a lot survives of buildings made of timber and thatch!'

'Any other finds?'

'Not that many. It was early in the Anglo-Saxon era so there was little "material culture". They probably didn't have a lot of stuff and what they did have was from wood, textiles, leather and horn.'

'Yes, the sort of materials that don't usually survive. 'By "early" do you mean pre-Christian?'

'Yes. Both the archaeology tells us that and the later history of Avebury.

'Just before we move off, take a look through this gap in the hedge at the next field. All those humps and bumps are from a surprisingly well-preserved water meadow.'

'Ah yes you were explaining those to me when we left West Kennett long barrow. So this little settlement was about as close to the Winterbourne as it could be without too much risk of being flooded?'

'Seems so. Let's just walk along the main path and look out for the sports field on our right.'

Grid reference 101698

'OK, so there's the cricket field. You're not trying to tell me that's

Under this part of the car park near the entrance was an early Anglo-Saxon settlement.

Anglo-Saxon?'

'Not at all. But this shallow bank running alongside the path just might be.

'Oh, yes, I'd not even noticed it till you said. But isn't it just something the groundsmen did when levelling the field?

'No! Because it's in exactly the right place to be part of the earthwork – the "bury" or burh in Old English – that gave Avebury it's name. And, if it is part of the burh it's the only part to have survived.

'When they used the word burh weren't they just referring to the huge ditches that we know as prehistoric?'

'Almost certainly not. Right through till at least the thirteenth century the prehistoric ditch and bank had the separate name of Waledich – which means the "wall ditch". And of course one of the other mega-henges is still known as Durrington Walls. So we can be fairly sure that the burh was the rectangular earthwork built just outside the "wall ditch".

'The burh's very hard to follow on the ground, but in the eighth century there must have been a fairly substantial bank

The field to the left of the car park entrance was once a water meadow which would have been intentionally flooded in early Spring; the village of Avebury Trusloe is on the higher ground beyond the Winterbourne.

and ditch that made a rectangle with curved corners enclosing several acres, with the newly-founded minster – the precursor to the parish church – inside.

'Just as a boundary?'

'Partly. But if there was a timber palisade on top, as there well might have been, then it would have been defensive too. It would have kept unwanted people out as well as unwelcome animals such as wolves and wild boars.

'If we follow this path to the High Street then turn a little to our right we'll see a wide path heading towards the National Trust café and shop. That probably more-or-less follows the line of the burh too, at the point where it incorporates the henge bank – though that's been dug away here. But it's more interesting not to go that way – turn left at the High Street and head for the church again.

Grid reference 100699

'But first just pause at the old village school that's now the social centre. Behind it is the 1970s school – although that's now become a children's nursery. When the school was

Avebury High Street and the western part of the henge, The rectangle with rounded rounded corners is the probable location of the Anglo-Saxon burh (defensive earthworks) around the minster (now the parish church. Only a small strech (to the east of 'B')) is now visible.

about to be built in the seventies there was a fairly big dig and it found evidence of Anglo-Saxon buildings. These were later that those at what's now the car park. They're inside the burh earthwork I was describing, so are perhaps where lay people working for the minster had their homes and workshops.'

''Shall we take a look?'

'Not a lot of point – it's just buildings and the little car park now.

'What intrigues me is that the second settlement is upstream of the earlier one, which is in turn upstream of the Roman town. We know from ethnography that it's often considered unlucky to build downstream and, as other Anglo-Saxon villages seem to migrate upstream too, then perhaps the Anglo-Saxons thought that way too.'

'Let me guess – you'd get drinking water upstream from where you emptied out your dirty water and more unmentionable what have you's. I can see that easily becoming a "superstition" that downstream is "unlucky".'

'Sounds good to me! Anyway let's see something that's really Anglo-Saxon instead of just talking about ideas. Head through the lychgate... '

'Yes, you said before that some of the church dates back to before the Norman Conquest in 1066. But does any of the church date back to the original minster.'

'Well, yes and no.

'A typical Bob answer that is!'

'Well there's something that dates back to the right time and it's now part of the church alright – but it's not part of the eighth century church.'

'Come on show me and explain!'

'Right make your way to the far side of the tower and look at what is strictly the north-west corner of the outside of the nave. Spot that rather decorative piece of stone?'

'Yes. Looks like it's a useful size piece of stone that's been reused from something else.'

'Correct! Imagine it stood on its end and – *voilà* – a fairly typical Anglo-Saxon cross-shaft of around the tenth century.'

Left: *So-called 'long and short work' in the north-west nave wall. This construction technique is unique to Anglo-Saxon buildings.*
Above: *Closer view of the early tenth century cross shaft fragment (visible near the bottom of the long and short work).*

This would have stood where – outside the original church?'

'Very likely. And it is also very likely that the first church – or even the first few churches – were wooden. But sometime nearer the eleventh century they rebuilt it in stone. This so-called "long-and-short work" just above the cross shaft fragment is typical of Anglo-Saxon building methods, but not

The south doorway.

done later on.'

'Is that all the Anglo-Saxon stuff?'

'No, there are three more fragments of tenth century decorative carving incorporated into the inside of the porch. And when we get inside the nave you'll see three round windows that go back before the Norman Conquest too.

'Interestingly, almost all the minsters in Wiltshire take their name from someone followed by the word burh. Presumably the person is the founding abbot who, after death, becomes something of a local saint. So Avebury might be Ava's burh. But if there was a "St Ava" – more likely to have been spelt "St Afa" at the time – then it's a woman's name. So, if this is a correct deduction – and the early forms of the name might suggest otherwise – then Avebury would have been founded not by an abbot but an abbess and she would have been head of a group of nuns. This is quite plausible as Heytsebury minster, over near Warminster, was named after a female founder, as were a few other minsters elsewhere in

Circular Anglo-Saxon windows in the north wall of the nave.

England.'

'You say the early forms of the place-name suggest otherwise. Why's that?'

'Well they seem to be corruptions of "avon burh" which simply means "river earthwork". In my opinion it simply doesn't work as a proper name – it's not distinctive enough. Most minsters were something –burh and for practical reasons needed to be near water. So lots of minsters could be thought of as an avon burh. Perhaps best just to leave the whole matter open!'

'And if we now go inside the church we can see some characteristically Anglo-Saxon round windows towards the top of the nave walls. But as we go through the porch just stop and take note of the south doorway.'

'With all the chevrons around it. That's typically Norman isn't it?'

'Yes. So twelfth century. We can also see another twelfth century doorway in the south side of the nave, although it has been badly cut away when the south arcade was built.'

'So the one now in the south porch must have been moved?'

'Yes. It might have been a west door which went when the

The twelfth century font with a bishop and two dragons – or are they wyverns? Not to mention a large bird perched on the back of one of the beasts.

tower was built.

'Anyway, those round windows in the top of the nave walls are the Anglo-Saxon ones, from about a hundred years or so before the Norman doorways.

'And then there's this wonderful Norman font. Come round to the west side… '

'Oh yes! That must be a bishop because he's holding a crozier. And he's literally been defaced. And there's a couple of dragons and all that wonderful stylised foliage.'

'Yes, it's known as "stiff leaf". Note that the dragons only have two legs so strictly we ought to call them wyverns. Although at the time it was carved people were as likely to refer to such monsters as Leviathans. And you've missed something…'

'What?'

'The big bird – perhaps it's an eagle or a raven – on the back on the left-hand "dragon".

'Just imagine that when this was new it would have been brightly – even a bit garishly – painted.

'Interestingly in 1086, at the time of the Domesday survey, this church was one of several run by a powerful clergyman called Regenbald. Clearly he would have been building up the sort of assets needed to rebuild the church and to commission such a font. It was probably one of his successors who did the work though.

'What about the rest of the church? Is there anything else interesting?'

'I'd say so. Look at the choir screen. It's said to be the best surviving pre-Reformation rood screen in Wiltshire, although obviously it's been restored.

'And the four musical angels all-but behind the altar are little gems. They're nineteenth century but rather splendid. Whoever did them was a better artists than the similar figures on the main reredos and on the restored choir screen.'

'Wasn't there also another religious institution here in the Middle Ages?'

'Ah, during reign of Henry I (1100–35) one of only two priories in England belonging to the abbey of St George de Boscherville, which is near Rouen, was founded at Avebury.'

'Do we know where?'

'Frankly, no. But the best guess is that when Henry VIII started shutting down almost all the monasteries and such like the priory was sold off to one of his mates. Typically they were converted into posh houses. There are some fairly complicated historical records for Avebury Manor around this time but they only refer to owners not building activities. But it is very likely that Avebury Manor incorporates part of that priory or, at the least, is on the site of it. But although folk have had a good look for old bits of masonry, there's no way of knowing for sure if anything is pre-Reformation.

'Certainly the manor house itself is outside the burh – even though the gardens now straddle that former boundary – so it's the right place for such a priory.'

'Let's just go back outside and go through the cobbled yard outside the Alexander Keiller Museum and head through the wrought iron gates.'

Grid reference 099700

'Nice avenue of trees!'

'Indeed. And to the left is the remains of yet another phase of Avebury – a medieval village which is all gone.

'And, once again, upstream!'

'Indeed. But then later everything contracts back to what is now called the High Street. The buildings near the crossroads and the Red Lion pub are all later and come about with regular coaching routes and then turnpikes.'

'And the contraction of the village is a result of the Dissolution of the two monastic sites.'

'Careful! The minster had evolved into a parish church by then. Whatever power it had around Domesday steady waned. The French-controlled priory would have been a very modest affair. So on the one hand the origins of Avebury are similar to a number of other places in the area which did evolve into modest sizes towns – Ramsbury would be a good example – but for some reason Avebury just didn't thrive. The best guess is that when the "new town" of Marlborough was planted on the edge of what had previously been the somewhat sleepy little settlement of Preschute then it took the trade and such like away from Avebury.'

'So it's as if these towns were competing with each other?'

'Indeed they were. And there were winners – such as Marlborough – and losers – such as Avebury and Yatesbury.'

'And I suppose that if Avebury wasn't so important for its prehistoric monuments, then it would be just another sleepy Wiltshire rural village.'

'And no one would be writing guide books about it! '

Return to the main car park via the path past the National Trust restaurant and shop. This follows the line of the minster's burh described on pages 132–3.

Acknowledgements

The nature of a guidebook means that it is not possible to include footnotes for all the ideas included. However all the published sources are listed in the following section. Much of my understanding of the prehistory of the Avebury area is based on the writings of Joshua Pollard and Mark Gillings (although they may well disagree with some of my 'elaborations'). My understanding of the Anglo-Saxon era is mostly based on the writings of Simon Draper, Bruce Eagles and Andrew Reynolds. Information about the Anglo-Saxon carvings in St James' church is taken from a national project led by Rosemary Cramp. Jim Leary and David Field's *The Story of Silbury Hill* is an exemplary book for making complex archaeological discoveries accessible to non-specialists. Mike Parker Pearson first suggested that Stonehenge was a place of the dead, and Alex Gibson elaborated this by suggesting henges might have been 'spirit traps'. Chris Gosden, Gary Lock, Joshua Pollard and Howard Williams have all explored 'the past in the past'. Chris Tilley first described the experience of approaching the henge along the West Kennett Avenue. Paul Devereux discovered the alignment of Windmill Hill with both the 'shelf' on Silbury Hill and West Kennett long barrow. Peter Knight has usefully brought together information about West Kennett long barrow. Andy Collins first published the ideas about the Cove, Cygnus, swans and souls. The information about Scottish Travellers comes from Sara Reith's discussions with Stanley Robertson.

The maps were drawn by Abby George who interpreted my rather vague brief exceptionally well. They are based on old Ordnance Survey maps with more modern features shown approximately. Archaeological information on these maps is based on a number of sources (mostly simplified to suit this guidebook). The map of the palisaded enclosures on page 92 is based on a survey published by English Heritage. Please note that all maps are only to assist with these walks and are not intended to be accurately to scale or complete in terms of either modern or prehistoric features.

My greatest debt is to Nick Snashall and Ros Cleal, respectively the archaeologist for the World Heritage Site and the curator of the Alexander Keiller Museum in Avebury. I learned much from their study days and one-to-one discussions, and greatly appreciate their encouragement and assistance. Ros very generously read through the first draft and made many helpful recommendations. However all the opinions – and any remaining errors – are mine. Ros also generously gave permission for the reproduction of the photographs used on pages 43, 45 (top left), 47, 59 and 66.

Helpful discussions and walks around the area include those with Andrew Collins, Jeremy Harte, Steve Marshall, the late Shaun Ogbourn, Christine Rhone, plus various 'members of the public' whose names I never knew with whom I have started conversations while out and about in the henge.

Perhaps I should also acknowledge Socrates for his Method. But I suspect he just gets the credit for a way of sharing ideas that could easily go back to the Neolithic or even before…

Finally, big thanks to Judi, without whom I would never have got to know the Avebury World Heritage Site so well or so enjoyably.

ſourceſ

Bayliss, Alex, Alasdair Whittle and Michael Wysocki, 2007, 'Talking about my generation: the date of the West Kennet long barrow', *Cambridge Archaeological Journal*, Vol. 17: 1 (supplement), p85–101.

Bek-Pedersen, Karen, 2011, *The Norns in Old Norse Mythology*, Dunedin.

Bradley, Richard, 1993, *Altering the Earth: The origins of monuments in Britain and continental Europe*, Society of Antiquaries of Scotland.

Bradley, Richard, 1998, *The Significance of Monuments: On the shaping of human experience in Neolithic and Bronze Age Europe*, Routledge.

Bradley, Richard, 2000, *An Archaeology of Natural Places*, Routledge.

Bradley, Richard, 2002, *The Past in Prehistoric Societies*, Routledge.

Brown, Graham, David Field and David McOrmish, 2004, *The Avebury Landscape: Aspects of the field archaeology of the Marlborough Downs*, Oxbow.

Cleal, Ros, 2008, *Avebury: Monuments and Landscape*, National Trust.

Collins, Andrew, 2008, *The Cygnus Mystery* (2nd end; 1st edn 2006), Watkins.

Devereux, Paul, 1991, 'Three-dimensional aspects of apparent relationships between selected natural and artificial features within the topography of the Avebury complex', *Antiquity*, Vol. 65, p894–8.

Draper, Simon, 2006, *Landscape, settlement and society in Roman and early Medieval Wiltshire* (BAR British series 419), Archaeopress.

Bruce Eagles, 2001, 'Anglo-Saxon presence and culture in Wiltshire c.AD450–c.675', in Ellis 2001.

Ellis, Peter (ed), 2001, *Roman Wiltshire and After*, Wiltshire Archaeological and Natural History Society.

Gibson, Alex, 2008, 'Were henges ghost traps?', *Current Archaeology*, 214, p34–9.

Gillings, Mark and Joshua Pollard, 2004, *Avebury*, Duckworth.

Gillings, Mark, Joshua Pollard, David Wheatley, and Rick Peterson, 2008, *Landscape of the Megaliths: Excavation and Fieldwork on the Avebury Monuments, 1997–2003*, Oxbow.

Gosden, Chris and Gary Lock, 1998, 'Prehistoric histories', *World Archaeology* 30:1, 2–12; online at www.scribd.com/doc/25418211/Prehistoric-Histories-Gosden

Ingold, Tim, 2000, *The Perception of the Environment: Essays on livelihood, dwelling and skill*, Routledge.

Knight, Peter, 2011, *West Kennett Long Barrow: Landscape, shamans and the cosmos*, Stone Seeker Publishing.

Lawson, Andrew, 2007, *Chalklands: An archaeology of Stonehenge and its region*, Hobnob.

Leary, Jim and David Field, 2010, *The Story of Silbury Hill*, English Heritage.

Oswald, A., C .Dyer and M. Barber, 2001, *The Creation of Monuments: Neolithic causewayed enclosures in the British Isles*, English Heritage.

Papworth, Martin, 2012, 'Geophysical survey of the northeast and southeast quadrants of Avebury henge, *Wiltshire Studies*, Vol. 105, p21–42.

Parker Pearson, Michael, and Ramilisonina, 1998, 'Stonehenge for the ancestors: the stones pass on the message'. *Antiquity*, Vol. 72, p308–26.

Parker Pearson, Michael, 2012, *Stonehenge: Exploring the greatest stone age mystery*, Simon and Schuster.

Pollard, Joshua (ed), 2008, *Prehistoric Britain*, Blackwell.

Pollard, Joshua and Andrew Reynolds, 2002, *Avebury: The biography of a landscape*, Tempus.

Powell, A.B., M J Allen and I Barnes, 1993, *Archaeology in the Avebury Area Wiltshire: Recent discoveries along the line of the Kennet Valley foul sewer pipeline* (Wessex Archaeology Report No. 6) Wessex Archaeology.

Reith, Sara, 2008 , 'Through the "eye of the skull": memory and tradition in a Travelling landscape', *Cultural Analysis*, Vol. 7; online at socrates.berkeley.edu/~caforum/volume7/pdf/reith.pdf

Robertson, Stanley, 1988, *Exodus to Alford*, Balnain Books.

Robertson, Stanley, 2009, *Reek Roon a Camp Fire*, Birlinn.

Simmonds, Sarah (ed), 2008, *Avebury World Heritage Site Values and Voices*, Kennet District Council.

Smith, Isobel F., 1965. *Windmill Hill and Avebury: Excavations by Alexander Keiller, 1925–1939*. Clarendon.

Smith, M., and M. Brickley, 2009, *People of the Long Barrows: Life, death and burial in the earlier Neolithic*, The History Press.

Tilley, Christopher, 1994, *A Phenomenology of Landscape*, Berg.

Tilley, Christopher, 2008, *Body and Image: Explorations in landscape phenomenology*, Left Coast Press.

Trubshaw, Bob, 2005, *Sacred Places Prehistory and popular imagination*, Heart of Albion.

Trubshaw, Bob, 2011, *Singing Up the Country: The songlines of Avebury and beyond*, Heart of Albion.

Trubshaw, Bob, 2012, *Spirits, Souls and Deities*, Heart of Albion; online at www.hoap.co.uk/general.htm#ssd

Singing Up
the Country

The songlines of Avebury
and beyond

Bob Trubshaw

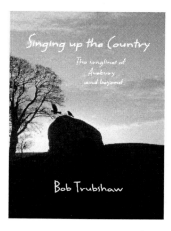

Singing Up the Country reveals that Bob
Trubshaw has been researching a
surprising variety of different topics
since his last book six years ago. From
Anglo-Saxon place-names to early Greek philosophy – and much in
between – he creates an interwoven approach to the prehistoric
landscape, creating a 'mindscape' that someone in Neolithic Britain
might just recognise. This is a mindscape where sound, swans and
rivers help us to understand the megalithic monuments.

Continuing from where scholarship usually stops and using instead
the approaches of storytelling, the final chapter weaves this wide
variety of ideas together as a 'songline' for the Avebury landscape.
This re-mythologising of the land follows two 'dreamtime' ancestors
along the Kennet valley to the precursors of Avebury henge and
Silbury Hill.

Few writers have Bob Trubshaw's breadth of knowledge combined
with a mythopoetic ability to construct a modern day story that re-
enchants the landscape. Singing Up the Country will be an
inspiration to all those interested in prehistory, mythology or the
Neolithic monuments of the World Heritage Site at Avebury.

> 'Trubshaw writes with practised and confident ease. His
> entertaining and sometimes jocular style makes for very easy
> reading; the experience is rather like sitting in a comfortable
> pub with a pint, listening to a seasoned storyteller.'
> Steve Marshall Fortean Times

ISBN 978-1-905646-21-0 2011. 245 x 175 mm, 189 + xiv pages, 64
b&w photos, 29 line drawings, paperback. **£14.95**

Sacred Places
Prehistory and popular imagination
Bob Trubshaw

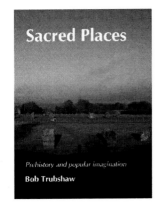

Sacred Places asks why certain types of prehistoric places are thought of as sacred, and explores how the physical presence of such sacred sites is less important than what these places signify. So this is not another guide book to sacred places but instead provides a unique and thought-provoking guide to the mental worlds – the mindscapes – in which we have created the idea of prehistoric sacred places.

Recurring throughout this book is the idea that we continually create and re-create our ideas about the past, about landscapes, and the places within those landscapes that we regard as sacred. For example, although such concepts as 'nature', 'landscape', 'countryside', 'rural' and the contrast between profane and sacred are all part of our everyday thinking, in this book Bob Trubshaw shows they are all modern cultural constructions which act as the 'unseen' foundations on which we construct more complex myths about places.

Key chapters look at how earth mysteries, modern paganism and other alternative approaches to sacred places developed in recent decades, and also outline the recent dramatic changes within academic archaeology. Is there now a 'middle way' between academic and alternative approaches which recognises that what we know about the past is far less significant than what we believe about the past?

> *'Sacred Places...* is a very valuable addition to the small body of thoughtful work on the spiritual landscapes of Great Britain and therefore recommended reading.'
> Nigel Pennick *Silver Wheel*

> 'One of the best books in the field I have ever read.'
> D J Tyrer *Monomyth Supplement*

ISBN 1 872883 67 2. 2005. 245 x 175 mm, 203 + xiv pages, 43 b&w illustrations and 7 line drawings, paperback. **£16.95**

'Highly recommended'
Folklore Society Katharine Briggs Award 2003

Explore Folklore

Bob Trubshaw

'A howling success, which plugs a big and obvious gap'

Professor Ronald Hutton

There have been fascinating developments in the study of folklore in the last twenty-or-so years, but few books about British folklore and folk customs reflect these exciting new approaches. As a result there is a huge gap between scholarly approaches to folklore studies and 'popular beliefs' about the character and history of British folklore. *Explore Folklore* is the first book to bridge that gap, and to show how much 'folklore' there is in modern day Britain.

Explore Folklore shows there is much more to folklore than morris dancing and fifty-something folksingers! The rituals of 'what we do on our holidays', funerals, stag nights and 'lingerie parties' are all full of 'unselfconscious' folk customs. Indeed, folklore is something that is integral to all our lives – it is so intrinsic we do not think of it as being 'folklore'.

Explore Folklore provides a lively introduction to the study of most genres of British folklore, presenting the more contentious and profound ideas in a readily accessible manner.

ISBN 1 872883 60 5. 2002. Demy 8vo (215x138 mm), 200 pages, illustrated, paperback **£9.95**

Stonehenge:
Celebration and Subversion

Andy Worthington

The story of the Stonehenge summer
solstice celebrations begins with the
Druid revival of the 18th century and
the earliest public gatherings of the 19th
and early 20th centuries. In the social
upheavals of the 1960s and early 70s,
these trailblazers were superseded by
the Stonehenge Free Festival. This
evolved from a small gathering to an
anarchic free state the size of a small
city, before its brutal suppression at the
Battle of the Beanfield in 1985.

In the aftermath of the Beanfield, the author examines how the political
and spiritual aspirations of the free festivals evolved into both the rave
scene and the road protest movement, and how the prevailing trends in
the counter-culture provided a fertile breeding ground for the
development of new Druid groups, the growth of paganism in general,
and the adoption of other sacred sites, in particular Stonehenge's
gargantuan neighbour at Avebury.

The account is brought up to date with the reopening of Stonehenge on
the summer solstice in 2000, the unprecedented crowds drawn by the
new access arrangements, and the latest source of conflict, centred on a
bitterly-contested road improvement scheme.

> '*Stonehenge Celebration and Subversion* contains an
> extraordinary story. Anyone who imagines Stonehenge to be
> nothing but an old fossil should read this and worry. [This
> book is] ... the most complete, well-illustrated analysis of
> Stonehenge's mysterious world of Druids, travellers, pagans
> and party-goers'. Mike Pitts *History Today*

ISBN 1 872883 76 1. 2004.   Perfect bound, 245 x 175 mm, 281 + xviii
pages, 147 b&w photos, **£14.95**

Heart of Albion

Publishing folklore, mythology and
local history since 1989

Further details of all Heart of Albion titles online at
www.hoap.co.uk

All titles available direct from Heart of Albion Press.
Please add £1.30 p&p (UK only; email **albion@indigogroup.co.uk**
for overseas postage).

To order books or request our current catalogue please contact

Heart of Albion Press

113 High Street, Avebury
Marlborough, SN8 1RF

Phone: 01672 539077

email: albion@indigogroup.co.uk
Web site: www.hoap.co.uk